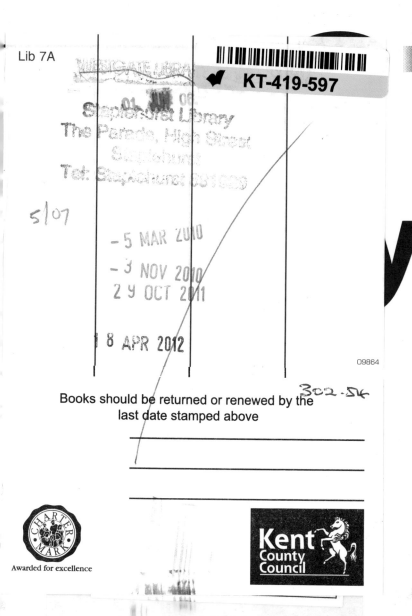

Awarded for excellence

Kent
County
Council

foulsham

LONDON • NEW YORK • TORONTO • SYDNEY

foulsham

The Publishing House, Bennetts Close, Cippenham, Slough, Berkshire, SL1 5AP, England

ISBN 0-572-03075-4

Cover photograph by Powerstock

A CIP record for this book is available from the British Library

Printed in Great Britain by Cox & Wyman Ltd, Reading, Berkshire

Contents

What Is Bullying?	5
How this Book Works	7
Our World of Energy	8
How Emotional Energy Vibrates	13
How Our Emotional Frequency Is Established	18
How Our Emotional Frequency Affects Our Lives	27
Frequency Variations	37
Taking Control	50
How Does Bullying Start?	58
Why Do They Pick on Me?	65
Where Bullying Happens and What Happens as a Result	67
Guidance for Parents	75
Techniques to Break the Cycle	79
Taking the Issue to the Comfort Zone	86
How Can I Help my Child?	91
If You Are the Bully ...	95
Three Steps to a Bully-free Life	97
Accepting Responsibility	100
Making the Commitment	102
Your Affirmations	107
Your Visualisations	111
My Progress to a Bully-free Life	119
Index	126

Dedicated to my mother, Janet,
and in loving memory of my brother, Jamie.

I love you.

What Is Bullying?

The definition of the verb 'to bully' in *The Oxford English Dictionary* is 'to inflict pain or hurt on another person for one's own gratification'.

Bullying takes many forms. Only rarely does it involve full-blown physical violence or serious mental abuse; far more often it takes the form of what, taken individually, might seem to be minor insults and harmless comments, but which, when they are constant and relentless, become something more aggressive. The common factor in all incidences of bullying is that the intention is to belittle and degrade another person.

Surveys show that bullying, in one form or another, is so prevalent in modern society that it probably affects everyone in some way. Whether it takes the form of physical violence in the playground or mental abuse in a relationship or the workplace, the results can be equally devastating. Indeed, statistics show that in 2003, 16 children in the UK took their lives as a result of bullying. In the workplace bullying costs millions of pounds every year through staff absences, illness, poor performance levels and lack of commitment.

Bullying is sometimes so subtle that we don't even realise we are being bullied. However, any situation in which someone else is making us feel bad about ourselves on a regular basis is bullying – and it can have a negative impact on many apparently unrelated aspects of our lives, even if we have not identified what is happening as bullying. Fundamentally, the bully is trying to demoralise and damage us, and, if they succeed, this can have wide-ranging repercussions. Being the victim of a bully puts us in a negative frame of mind, and this may not only make us feel unhappy but also put a strain on our relationships, affect our standard of work and create complications throughout our life.

You might be surprised to learn that the same also goes for the bully. Not infrequently, the bully doesn't even realise what they are doing and would be surprised and mortified to learn that they are using bullying behaviour. Bullying damages the bully as well as the bullied, so it is in everyone's interests to stop it.

If you, or someone close to you, is being bullied – or if you recognise that you may be a bully – it is vital to do something to put a stop to it as soon as possible, before any long-lasting damage can be done. And that's where high-vibrational thinking comes in, because it will help you to do just that.

How this Book Works

The first section of this book explains what high-vibrational thinking is and how it works.

The second section shows you how to use high-vibrational thinking to stop the bully who is harassing you. Using high-vibrational thinking – or HVT – will first of all give you a much clearer picture of exactly what is happening in your life. No matter how subtle or cunning the bully's tactics, it will shed a very revealing light, enabling you to see clearly where bullying is taking place. Once you recognise bullying for what it is, you can start to understand how and why it is happening. That puts you in control – and taking control is the first step on the way to stopping bullying in its tracks and opening the door to a new life without bullying.

Our World of Energy

'If you want to find the secrets of the universe, think in terms of energy, frequency and vibration.' Dr Nikola Tesla, 1942

Dr Nikola Tesla was one of the foremost scientists of the early twentieth century. His outstanding intellect paved the way for a large number of modern technological developments; in fact the tesla coil is still used in many television sets today. It is amazing to think that his words in 1942 should be still so relevant today. We now know that his understanding of the universe as energy, frequency and vibration was quite accurate. As we explore the intricate workings of the universe, unlocking the secrets of this amazing world of energy in which we live, this fact only becomes clearer.

Nothing you see around you is quite as it seems! The world that we live in is a huge ocean of energy, taking many different forms. The age of the microscope has shown us abundantly clearly that things that appear solid and static to us are in fact nothing of the sort. Even if the only science you know has been learnt from TV dramas about forensic scientists, you will be aware that if you look at an apparently solid object at a sufficiently powerful magnification, you will find that it is made up not of a single solid substance but of tiny particles vibrating at phenomenal speed. These tiny particles are known as neutrons, electrons and protons, and they link together to form atoms, the most basic building blocks of life.

What is perhaps even more astonishing is that atoms actually consist of 90 per cent empty space, which – by logical deduction – means that what we think of as solid, such as a concrete wall, is in fact mostly not solid at all! Nothing around us is actually solid, even though it may appear so; everything is made up of energy, vibrating constantly and at various frequencies. This applies to everything you see around you: trees, houses, cars, walls, roads, dogs, cats, fish. It is a fundamental law of physics and applies even to us humans.

Each of these millions upon millions of different forms of energy vibrates at a specific frequency. The frequency at which it vibrates influences the form of the object. For example, the molecules of a solid vibrate very slowly; the molecules of a liquid vibrate more quickly; and the molecules of a gas vibrate even more quickly. Thus something with the same chemical composition can take different forms depending on the vibrational frequency of its molecules. When the molecules are vibrating at a medium frequency rate, water appears as a liquid. Slow down that frequency and you get ice; speed up the frequency and you get steam.

We are all part of the vibrant ocean of energy
As I have said, we are just as much a part of this cycle of energy as everything else around us. High-vibrational thinking is based on that fact. Its fundamental principal is that we need to learn to see and think about our world in terms of energy.

High-vibrational thinking is a revolutionary new concept that teaches us how to have some control over the incredible universe of energy that we live in. It offers a way of seeing people – and the interactions between people – as part of a unique energy transmission process that is hugely empowering to the individual. The first part of this book explains exactly how the system works. If you go back to fundamentals, it is really very easy to understand.

Just as ice, water and steam vibrate at different frequencies, so emotional energy also vibrates at different frequencies. As I will be explaining in detail later, positive emotions are high-vibrational energies, while negative emotions are low-vibrational energies. If we can find a way to maintain high-vibrational energy and deflect low-vibrational energy, then we can change our whole perspective on life. That's what HVT can help us to do. HVT is a system that takes positive thinking into an exciting new dimension.

HVT changes your perspective

This realisation throws a whole new light on how we perceive our world. Indeed, knowing how to use this information – and I'll be showing you that too – can be hugely liberating and empowering, because it offers a way of using our knowledge to handle our lives in a more beneficial and productive way. This new perspective gives you far greater control over everyday situations and events that you may previously have thought were largely beyond your control. With this knowledge comes power, and that power is the ability to choose more carefully how you relate to the energies that affect your life.

HVT will become automatic

What's more, once you have learnt how to use this power, it will become an automatic way of thinking, and you can gain the benefits without even having to make a conscious choice about it. Once you have learnt to walk, you don't need to think consciously about the process any more. It's the same with HVT. Once you understand HVT, you will find that you automatically begin to incorporate it into your life as a working practice without any conscious effort on your part. Its positive influence on your life will be automatic, as the truth of HVT, once learnt, cannot be ignored. Using HVT on a daily basis becomes a natural habit that will benefit every aspect of your life and help you to change in a positive and fulfilling way. All of a sudden, you will find that something inside you is monitoring the events and situations in your life and automatically responding to negative situations in a way that will prevent them from dragging down the frequency of your energy field and making you feel bad.

A paradigm shift in consciousness occurs when you use HVT. You find yourself able to deal with the negative events and situations that are part of everyday life in a new and positive way. HVT enables you to take control of events and situations rather than allowing them to control you. This is incredibly liberating, freeing your mind to direct your life in a much more productive and focused way.

Let's look at a simple example from an HVT course I recently ran. Within days of attending the course, two of my students found themselves turning off a particular television programme that they had been watching regularly for many years. They did not think about this action consciously until weeks later when it came up in conversation. Another student was talking about how negative this television programme had become. At that point, they both realised they had made the decision not to watch it any more immediately after attending the HVT course. Subconsciously they had sensed its negative impact and put a stop to it.

This kind of reaction is common among people who attend HVT courses, because they quickly learn to avoid engaging with damaging negative energies. You are already starting to learn that lesson simply by reading this book.

You too can learn automatically to handle situations and decisions in a more positive and beneficial way.

Essentially simple

The real strength of HVT is its simplicity and the fact that when applied to any subject it breaks it down to a few basics. This enables anybody, whatever their age or background, to gain an understanding that previously may have seemed impossible. This is one of the reasons we have had so much success in working with children as young as ten years old. Young people absorb the concept very quickly and find it easy to think in terms of HVT about every area of their life.

It also means that the technique can be applied to any aspect of your life, regardless of your occupation or lifestyle. At school, it can give your more confidence and enthusiasm and help you to perform well. At work, it can cut out negativity, create a better atmosphere and even increase productivity. In the home, it can reduce arguments and create a more loving environment.

Essentially, HVT is about making you feel good about yourself and maintaining that feel-good factor whatever life throws at you. Just think how much happier that could make you – not to mention the immeasurable stride forwards in terms of moving our world into a brighter, high-vibrational future.

How Emotional Energy Vibrates

Now we understand that the whole world is part of a complex energy system, let's look specifically at how that affects us. Here, we are talking in terms of the power of emotional energy, and that is what we can harness to work to our advantage with HVT.

We have seen that – just like the objects around us – we are made up of energy and – like all forms of energy – our personal energy field vibrates constantly. The vibrational frequency of our energy field is affected by our thoughts and feelings. These are also made up of energy waves, and they influence our lives much more profoundly than we may realise. So depending on how we are feeling at any given time, the frequency at which our energy field vibrates can change dramatically.

Scientists and researchers in the USA have measured the frequency of the energy waves transmitted by the emotion of love, which they found vibrate very quickly, or at a very high frequency. Similarly, they measured the frequency of the energy waves transmitted by the emotion of fear, which they found vibrate very slowly, or at a low frequency. Our world exists within these two parameters.

Love is transmitted on a short wavelength, so it has a fast, high-vibrational frequency.

Fear is transmitted on a long wavelength, so it has a slow, low-vibrational frequency.

Think for a moment about listening to the radio, and this will help you to understand how energy waves work. Radio stations are constantly transmitting radio waves. These are in the air all around us, even though we cannot actually see them. If your radio is not tuned in to the right frequency, all you will hear is an annoying hiss. However, if you tune in your radio to the right frequency, you will be able to pick up on those radio waves so that you can hear and understand them perfectly, whether they are transmitting music, news, drama or comedy.

Happy is a high vibration
So whatever we are thinking and feeling has a very real effect, as it alters the frequency of our personal energy field. If we are happy, our energy is high-vibrational; if we are sad, our energy is low-vibrational. I am sure you are already getting the idea. Similarly, we can be affected by other people's thoughts and feelings. If you are unlucky enough to be in a room full of bored or unhappy people, it is very hard to remain upbeat and cheerful.

When we are full of laughter and joy, it makes us feel good. What is actually happening is that the high-vibrational energy of joy has pushed up the frequency of our personal energy field. We also experience this effect when we achieve something good, such as passing a driving test or an exam, scoring a goal, winning a competition, or receiving praise for a job well done. What is happening here is the same: the achievement has made us feel suddenly successful and good about ourselves, again pushing up the frequency of our personal energy field.

So, as you can see, any thoughts and feelings that are positive – laughter, joy, honesty, sincerity, truth, compassion – are high-vibrational, keeping our energy field vibrating at the higher levels and therefore making us feel good. Just think about some of the expressions we use to describe that kind of feeling: 'I'm high as a kite', 'I'm buzzing', 'My mind's racing'. They are referring to the frequency of our personal energy field, and they clearly demonstrate that wonderful elation. The faster our energy field vibrates, the better we feel, because that means we are closer to the frequency of love.

Of course, the opposite is also true. Anger, frustration, hate, jealousy, envy, greed and selfishness are all negative thoughts and feelings. Such emotions are low-vibrational; they slow down our energy field and make us feel bad. This is why we use phrases such as 'I'm down in the dumps' or 'I'm flat as a pancake'. The lower our energy field vibrates, the closer we are to the vibration of fear – which is not where we want to be!

Increasing our vibrational frequency

Even though this may be the first time you have thought about it in these terms, you will probably recognise that we spend most of our time trying to feel good about ourselves. In HVT terms, that means we are constantly seeking to increase our vibrational energy frequency.

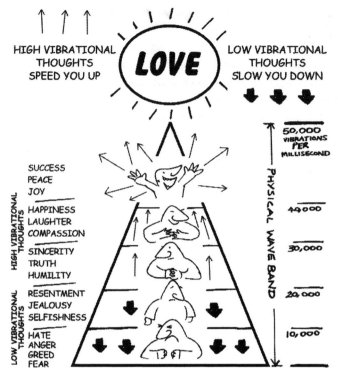

*Hypothetically speaking, the physical waveband may run from
0 to 50,000 vibrations per millisecond. Our energy fields
fluctuate between these parameters in our day-to-day lives.
When we are happy and enjoying life, we may be vibrating at
35,000 vibrations per millisecond, but this may fall to 6,000
vibrations per millisecond when we are down in the dumps.*

There are any number of ways to try to do this – getting
your hair done, buying new clothes, having a drink, going
to the gym, planning a special night out. They can all be
effective, but if they don't alter your fundamental
emotional state, the effect is not going to last very long. If
you have ever got a buzz from buying a new pair of shoes,
only to feel low again by the time you got home because

you had nowhere to go to show them off, you'll know what I mean.

Some people take the search for a high to extremes, experimenting with drink and drugs. This may give a temporary 'high' but can very soon have the serious negative result of addiction.

That's where HVT comes in, because it is a way of educating ourselves so that our normal vibrational frequency is higher – plus it teaches us to control the effects of low-vibrational energy from other sources. It's just like exercising regularly to increase your resting heart rate. This not only makes you feel fitter but it also makes it easier for you to cope with the physical demands of your everyday life.

How Our Emotional Frequency Is Established

As we spend most of our time trying to raise our vibrational frequency in order to feel better about ourselves, it makes sense to have a look at the factors that determine our individual energy level in the first place. This energy level is established and controlled primarily by our subconscious mind.

The conscious and subconscious mind

Your conscious mind is what you use to go about your everyday life – paying the bills, cleaning, sorting the washing, going to work. This is the methodical, reasoning part of your mind that carries out the daily tasks. It is the organised, sensible, logical part of you that understands how your world works. Your conscious mind automatically analyses any situation it confronts and plots the best and most logical way to deal with it.

Your subconscious mind, on the other hand, is a more complex entity, and is a source of immense power. It is affected by your surroundings in much more subtle ways and reacts most strongly to emotional stimuli.

Many psychologists refer to the subconscious mind as the 'inner child', because they feel that this best describes its characteristics. This terminology can help us to understand why our subconscious can sometimes pull us towards something that is not good for us. Imagine yourself as a child of five years old, with all the feelings and wonderment you had at that age; now imagine that this child is real and living inside you. Now you have a picture of your subconscious mind. It does not reflect you as you are now, with everything you have experienced and learnt over the course of a lifetime, but you as you were then. This child has no concept of what is good or bad for

Your inner child (your subconscious mind) will do everything it can to keep you in your comfort zone, even if this means holding you back in your life.

you; it just has its programming, which it will try to stick to regardless of what you may or may not consciously want.

In other words, we are all going through life trying to make some kind of progress but subject to the limitations that our subconscious mind places upon us. In terms of energy, our subconscious monitors us on a daily basis to keep us in what it has defined as our normal vibrational frequency zone.

Our formative years

The most important factor in determining this normal or average vibrational frequency level is the first five or six years of our lives. It is during these formative years that we establish our general thought patterns about ourselves. These first five or six years effectively programme our subconscious mind with certain beliefs about ourselves, which we then carry throughout the rest of our lives and which are very difficult to change. This vibrational frequency programming sets the boundaries for us and has a major bearing on every aspect of our life from then on.

The most influential factors in our development are our immediate family and the environment we grow up in. In other words, the vibrational frequency of our environment and the frequency level of our family are what we pick up and become used to as our norm. When our mind is young and impressionable during those early years, we readily accept the situation in which we find ourselves. Because we don't know of any other situation, we unquestioningly believe that this is where we belong. This becomes the frequency zone we feel comfortable in and which, subconsciously, we spend virtually the rest of our lives trying to stay in.

So if you were brought up in a family with not much love (high-vibrational energy), you will believe that you only deserve a certain amount of love in your life, and your subconscious will use all its power to make sure that that is what happens. This will have massive repercussions, affecting your relationships, your work – in fact, everything you do in life. Your subconscious will stick to the programming, whether it's good for you or bad for you. In other words, it will monitor your vibrational frequency and keep it at the level that it is programmed to do.

As we grow up, our subconscious beliefs tend to become self-confirming because we constantly play them over in our subconscious mind, reaffirming our opinions and thoughts about ourselves. Most of the time, we are completely unaware that we are doing this. When we are constantly affirming to ourselves that we are not worthy (worthy meaning deserving of love, the highest-vibrational energy), we are keeping our vibrational frequency at the lower levels – and making life much harder for ourselves. The opposite is also true. If we constantly circulate high-vibrational thoughts about ourselves, we will keep our vibrational frequency at the higher levels, which in turn affirms that we are worthy and makes our life run much more smoothly.

Your inner child (subconscious mind) is much more in control of your life than you realise.

Of course, we have to acknowledge that we are all different and unique individuals with many varying factors determining our personality. This is why different people emerge from a similar upbringing with a different attitude to life. However, you are almost certainly reading this book because at least one aspect of your life can be improved, and understanding where any negative input may have come from is the first step towards being able to change the negative and maximise the positive.

The comfort zone

The energy level that we feel is where we belong is often referred to as our 'comfort zone'. We find it very difficult to break out of this zone, as our subconscious mind constantly draws us back to it as its starting point, regardless of whether it is in fact good for us or bad for us. This may seem strange but is in fact quite logical.

We tend to mix and feel more comfortable with people of a similar vibration rate.

You may, for example, feel uncomfortable in an upmarket, expensive restaurant, or perhaps you feel nervous when talking to professional people such as lawyers or consultants. What you are experiencing is a reaction to the frequency of the environment or person – if the frequency is vibrating at a higher rate than yours, you will probably feel slightly uncomfortable. This means you will seek out places and people with which you share a similar frequency, as this is where you naturally feel most comfortable.

Imagine carrying around with you an identity card that has not only all your personal details but also all your unconscious beliefs about yourself printed on it. If your normal vibrational frequency is low, your ID might list some of the following:

▸ You will only be shown a limited amount of affection from people who are close to you
▸ You are only allowed to have a low-paid job
▸ You are only allowed to live in a small house
▸ You are only allowed to have an old car
▸ You are only allowed to be average in what you do
▸ You are only allowed to wear casual clothes
▸ You will only be able to achieve a limited amount of success
▸ You will only ever have difficult relationships
▸ You will only ever have friends who take advantage of you

Now imagine that if you try to step out of line by going against these guidelines, you will be confronted by a police officer whose job it is to keep you within their confines. Let's say you manage to get a good job that pays well. Before you know it, the officer is on your case and starts talking you out of the job. You may find that you can't motivate yourself to raise your level of achievement as you need to in order to do the job well, so you start to make excuses and lay the blame elsewhere. Instead, you tell yourself that you work too hard or the firm is taking advantage of you, the pay is not adequate or you are not appreciated. This undermines your confidence and your ability to do the job well, and before very long you will find a way to give up the job while blaming everyone else.

I have seen this happen in my own experience. A very capable employee suddenly, after about three months in the job, begins to under perform. They start coming in late with any old feeble excuse, they cultivate an attitude of not been appreciated, they disrupt the other staff and in the end they push you so far that you have no choice but to let them go. When this happens, they insist that they are being victimised, they have done nothing wrong, and they may even threaten to take you to a tribunal. What they fail to acknowledge – even to themselves – is that it is their own behaviour that has caused the problem. The police officer has done his job and dragged them back into their low-vibrational comfort zone.

The problem with this situation is that we don't realise what is happening – that it is our own subconscious mind that is wreaking such havoc in our lives. It does not seem logical to believe that we would sabotage our own efforts, so we assume that the fault lies elsewhere.

I have experienced this myself, so I know how easily it can occur. When I was at school I was quite good at sport and soon found myself playing for the school teams. I did very well, and at one point it was expected that I might go on to a higher level. Once I realised that this was in prospect, I couldn't seem to motivate myself any more and decided to stop playing altogether. At the time, I just decided that I didn't feel like playing any more; it was only years later that I realised what had taken place. The threat of success had triggered off my subconscious programming, which dictated that I didn't deserve the high-frequency feelings that success could bring. These would have pushed me out of my comfort zone and into a new higher-frequency zone, so my subconscious mind convinced me that I didn't like sports any more and made me feel tired and unmotivated when faced with a game. Unfortunately for me, my subconscious won, and at 14 years of age I hung up my boots and as a result missed many years of enjoyment.

Not better but different

One thing always to remember, however, is that even if you start out with a low-vibrational energy field and feel uncomfortable with a different group of people, they are not 'better' than you. We all have our own qualities, strengths and weaknesses. You may want to be more like someone who has a high-vibrational energy field because they are fun to be around and are positive and more successful – that's fine. But that doesn't make them intrinsically better than you. Envy and self-criticism are both low-vibrational emotions, and if you give way to them, it will only make things worse.

You may, on the other hand, be someone who has had a good upbringing in a high-vibrational environment, leaving you with high-vibrational thought patterns. This gives you a much better chance of making the most of your life and better equips you to take advantage of opportunities that arise. You may still feel uncomfortable in places or with people where the energy pattern does not match your own – probably because your personal energy field is vibrating at a higher frequency – but it is important that you do not fall into the trap of believing that this makes you better in some way, for this is a damaging thought pattern. Arrogance and self-importance will pull down your energy frequency.

Don't try to place blame

It is important to point out here that your parents and their parents before them were also subject to this subconscious programming. However they brought you up, they were doing their best within their own programmed mental confines.

It is essential that you do not try to attach blame to anybody for your life as it stands at the moment. This would be to go straight down the low-vibrational route. Such thought processes are negative and low-frequency; they are certain to act as a dead weight around your neck and pull you down. Pointing the finger at others serves no purpose and will only harm you – by lowering your vibrational frequency. This is the time to assess the past and move on to the new, high-vibrational you.

How Our Emotional Frequency Affects Our Lives

The easiest way to demonstrate how limiting it can be to allow your subconscious mind to remain in control of your life is to take a look at a few examples.

Paul's comfort zone with crime

A few years ago, my work brought me into contact with a sales representative who proceeded to tell me a bit about himself. Let's call him Paul. Paul was brought up in a fairly tough environment, and his father had not been around much, as he had spent most of his time in prison for relatively minor offences. However, this childhood grounding had taken its toll, and, at 12 years old, Paul had found himself in trouble with the police for the first time for a minor crime. His family considered crime as a profession and accepted it as a normal way of life so, far from chastising him for having committed a crime, they were more concerned that he had not got away with it. This pathway continued. Paul's teenage years were littered with offences, but since he was behaving exactly according to his own idea of normality, he could see nothing unacceptable in this.

At the age of 25, during another stay in prison, Paul decided to go straight. He left prison with good intentions, found himself a job and at first managed to stay on the straight and narrow. It wasn't long, however, before he found himself drawn back to crime, even though he tried not to be tempted. When I spoke to him, he was very disappointed with himself and said that no matter how hard he tried, he kept finding himself committing offences. Although this made him feel bad about himself, when the temptation was there, he just could not resist it.

I wish I could tell you that this story has a happy ending, but I lost contact with Paul many years ago and do not know how his life has turned out. However, over the years, I have given Paul's story a great deal of thought. When I began to understand the workings of the subconscious mind, it became clear to me exactly what his problem was. Even though Paul wanted to stop being drawn to crime, his subconscious mind (inner child) did not. To his subconscious mind, crime was defined as normal behaviour – because this is what it had been programmed with during his first five or six years – and so was safely in his comfort zone. When, as an adult, Paul wanted to break out of his comfort zone, his subconscious mind took every opportunity to draw him back in.

When you think about how deep-rooted and fundamental our subconscious mind is to our entire personality, it is hardly surprising that it is very influential. We all have to contend with the daily tussle with our subconscious mind, but when we understand that it is simply trying to keep us within the boundaries of our own comfort zone, we have taken the first step towards doing something to take control over it.

Sue's comfort zone with food
Another friend of mine – let's call her Sue – has spent the last year or so trying to lose weight – something many of us have struggled with at some time. She has tried every

kind of diet, with the same results: she loses a few pounds at the beginning, but a few weeks later the weight is back on. Then it's on to the next diet regime. She has fallen into the trap of yoyo dieting and is unable to maintain her ideal weight for any length of time. So why is it so difficult for Sue – like many of us – to get into new eating habits and stick to them?

Let's take a careful look at what is happening here. When Sue begins the diet, she really wants to lose weight and is fully motivated. She has the necessary willpower to control her eating habits. She knows that she will feel better and be healthier if she eats well and maintains the right weight for her height and build. The principles are easy enough to understand: eat the right amount of the right foods and she will lose weight. And with the range of healthy food options available these days, there is never even any need for her to feel hungry. Nevertheless, after the first few weeks, or even days, she finds herself drifting back into bad eating habits. Sue's favourite tactic is to move the goal posts. Having decided that she wanted to lose weight for an up-and-coming holiday, she then decides it's for her daughter's graduation ceremony, then for Christmas, then for the new year, and so on.

The problem is, of course, that Sue is obeying her inner child. Her subconscious is telling her that the unhealthy diet she has become used to or has cultivated over the years is what she should be eating. This kind of food is her comfort zone, and it is very difficult to leave it. 'No, you can't have any chocolate or sweets and you must eat plenty of fresh vegetables' isn't what Sue's inner child wants to hear. Sue's initial determination will control the child for a while, but very soon the child's persistence will be rewarded, because it just feels right to go back to your comfort zone.

Jim's comfort zone with keeping fit

Jim's story is another good example of how the subconscious mind sabotages our efforts to instigate change. When Jim first went to the gym he was filled with enthusiasm and energy for his get-fit project. Sure enough, the first few visits were easy, as he raced around the equipment, lifting weights, doing sit-ups and so on, quite possibly overdoing it in his eagerness to succeed. Then, after a while, the novelty wore off. Jim started to accept the feeblest excuses for not going to the gym – 'I have to take the dog for a walk', 'I feel a bit tired' and (an old favourite of many of us) 'I haven't got time'. Of course, just as Jim's initial determination had begun to wear off, his subconscious mind had kicked in, renewing its bid to regain control and pull Jim back into his comfort zone.

Your subconscious mind acts just like a child and soon gets bored.

Just imagine taking a five-year-old child to the gym with you. At first they may be excited and full of energy, dragging you around the gym and trying out all the equipment. This might continue for two or three visits, but then the child would begin to get bored and start whingeing about having to go. You would end up virtually dragging them there, and while you doggedly followed your keep-fit programme, the child would probably be sitting in the corner sulking.

This is exactly what happens in reality; only it's your inner child that behaves in this way. You don't realise that this is what is going on; you just feel the symptoms. Your enthusiasm wanes, you feel tired, you look for excuses not to go, and the next thing you know, you haven't been for weeks and you regret taking out a gym membership that commits you to the next – very expensive – six months.

Familiar story? I know it's happened to me on more than one occasion. Yet again, it's the subconscious mind dragging us back into our comfort zone – no wonder it is so hard to go forward in life when the most restricting factor is hidden in our own head. But remember, knowing what's going on is the first step towards being able to do something about it.

Jeff and Dave's stories

Another way to explore the notion of the comfort zone is to compare two people with similar upbringings. Jeff and Dave had known each other all their lives. They grew up together on a housing estate in a typical working-class environment. Their birthdays were only three days apart, and as children they were inseparable.

Jeff was the youngest of five children, with two brothers and two sisters. Life was quite hard for them, as their father and mother had separated when Jeff was only five years old, and during the time before the separation the house had been filled with arguments and anger as his parents struggled to cope. Jeff's father had never held down a job for long and spent most of his time drinking and gambling away the family's money on the horses. Money was therefore scarce, and Jeff had to rely on hand-me-down clothes from his older brothers. The family always had enough to eat, but there was no money for life's luxuries, such as holidays, treats or days out. All these factors combined to mean that the primary emotions surrounding Jeff in his formative years were anger, worry, self-pity, hostility, fear and a general sense of having less than everybody else.

As you will now recognise, all these emotions are low-vibrational. Naturally, they contributed hugely to how Jeff felt about himself. He felt that he wasn't as good as most of the other children because they seemed to have lots more than him, so his habitual thought patterns about himself were low-frequency: 'I don't deserve', 'I'm not as good as other people' and 'I can't do anything' were the kind of statements he would unconsciously repeat to himself. This negativity became Jeff's norm. His subconscious mind believed this was what he deserved to be, and it set about ensuring that this was what he got for the rest of his life.

Jeff was a very good soccer player and made the school team, but he found it hard to motivate himself and missed many chances of furthering his progress. He was quite bright but somehow could never be bothered to try hard enough, so he failed most of his exams. He could have made the swimming team but found an excuse so that he didn't have to take part.

When he left school, Jeff found work with an insurance company as a sales representative. He did okay, but somehow he was never going to be one of the high flyers. After a few years in this job he decided that selling insurance was too much like hard work and that he would do much better in a new job, even though some of the other reps were making good money and doing very well. He always had his own reasons for why they did better than him. It was because they had better areas than him or easier policies to sell. One thing was for sure: it was never his fault. So Jeff continued moving from one job to the next over the next few years, not really getting on in any of them, because – according to Jeff – the other reps always had it better in some way. In the end, he put it down to the fact that he just didn't have any luck.

The crucial fact that Jeff wasn't aware of was that he himself was in control of his seeming lack of good fortune. His subconscious mind – programmed to believe that Jeff

Dave and Jeff had totally different outlooks on life: Dave was positive, Jeff was negative.

deserved to stay at a low frequency level – was monitoring his life all the way along. In order to keep him at his frequency level, it 'allowed' him only a very small amount of success – any more would have pushed him into a higher frequency zone. As soon as it looked as if he might become more successful, his subconscious mind kicked in and sabotaged any possibility of that happening. A little voice in Jeff's head would convince him that somebody had it in for him or he never got a fair chance or he should find another job because nobody in his current company appreciated him. This is how our subconscious mind keeps us within the comfort zone that it is programmed for.

Now let's take a look at Dave. Dave was an only child whose parents doted on him. His father was a foreman at the local steel works and his mother a very loving woman who spent her time looking after the family and their home. Dave's home was filled with love and positive energy. He remembers that his parents very rarely argued or had any kind of disagreement. Dave grew up a very happy child, whose parents gave him lots of attention and constantly told him that they loved him. Being an only child, he wanted for nothing. He always had fashionable clothes, and there were holidays abroad every year.

Growing up in this pleasant, loving, high-vibrational environment programmed Dave's subconscious mind to believe that this was the frequency zone in which he belonged. His habitual thought patterns about himself were positive: 'I know I can do it', 'I deserve the best', 'I am as good as anybody'.

Dave was never quite as good at soccer as Jeff, but he worked hard and with conviction, so he progressed further and made it to junior colts level with the local professional soccer club. Dave was not quite as bright as Jeff, but, again, he worked hard and eventually left school with good qualifications. After school, Dave followed Jeff into the insurance business and also became a sales representative. He always came in among the top two or three sales reps in the area. He loved his job, and his attitude impressed the management. He was soon promoted to area sales manager, then a few years later to regional sales director. Dave's life seemed charmed compared to Jeff's; everything always seemed to work out for him.

Jeff and Dave's friendship suffered over the years as their different life paths moved them into different social circles. Of course, they still spoke when they met, but after a while they found they had little in common, and their meetings became more of a passing hello than an in-depth conversation. In fact, Dave's success engendered not a little resentment in Jeff, which, sadly, estranged the two men even further.

Why our vibrational frequency is so important

Looking at Dave and Jeff's lives gives us an idea of how incredibly important our early years are in determining how easy the rest of our life is likely to be. Even though Dave was less talented and not as bright as Jeff, it was still much easier for him to be successful in life than it was for Jeff.

Dave's subconscious programming was of a much higher frequency than Jeff's. His feelings about himself and his own expectations were on a more high-vibrational frequency. He felt better about his abilities, so he had the confidence to try harder; he expected the best, so he impressed others with his positive attitude. All this enabled him to be successful at most of the things that he attempted. His subconscious mind monitored his life and kept him in the higher-frequency zone where it was programmed to believe he should be.

This meant that Dave saw life in a very different way from Jeff. What appeared to be insurmountable obstacles to

Dave had a much more high-frequency upbringing than Jeff,
and this was the real difference between them.

Jeff were mere molehills to Dave. In a situation where
Jeff's subconscious mind might say, 'That's just my luck; it
will never work out for me', Dave's would say 'I'm always
lucky; I know this will work for me'. Where Jeff's
subconscious might say 'This job is a waste of time;
everybody has an insurance policy', Dave's might say, 'I
love this job; everybody needs insurance'. At higher
frequency levels, life looks and feels completely different
than it does at the lower levels. Jeff and Dave had exactly
the same job, dealing with the same customers, and they
had the same potential for success; the only difference was
their vibrational frequency.

By now you will have a very clear idea of how our
personal vibrational frequency can control our lives. You
will soon begin to learn how high-vibrational thinking can
help to change that frequency and put us back in control.

Frequency Variations

Before we move on to looking at how to start raising your vibrational frequency, there is one more issue to consider. That is how our average vibrational frequency changes naturally. Although it is true that the foundations of our subconscious, and therefore our average frequency level, are established at an early stage, our frequency level can and does change in relation to time, the people we interact with and the various challenges life presents us with.

We regularly encounter both high-vibrational and low-vibrational energy from both inside and outside. Here we are going to look at the energy we encounter from outside. How we cope with this on the inside is, of course, vital, so we'll look at this issue at the end of the chapter.

Frequency interaction

How we interact with other people has a major impact on our energy levels on a daily basis. In the case of Jeff and Dave in the previous chapter, we saw that Dave had a fundamentally positive, high-frequency energy, and because of this he made other people feel better too. The management recognised his potential, the customers were more responsive. This is because any interaction with another human being affects your frequency level. If you interact with somebody of a higher frequency, you will have your frequency pulled up; likewise, if you interact with a person of a lower frequency, you will be dragged down. This is why some people feel very draining to be with, whereas others feel uplifting.

A positive, high-frequency attitude is great to be around.

It's easy to demonstrate this effect just by thinking about a few of the people you know. If you are having a conversation with someone who is up-beat and enthusiastic, there's lots of high-vibrational energy around. You can chat for hours without the conversation lagging. On the other hand, if you are having a conversation with someone who is withdrawn and unhappy, there's so much low-vibrational energy that you may struggle to keep the conversation going. You are being affected by this person's low-vibrational energies – as they are likewise affected by your vibrational frequency.

Let's pursue this a bit further. If you are yourself feeling down while you are trying to cheer someone else up, it will be much harder work. In fact, it's quite likely that you will both ending up crying into your beer! On the other hand, if you are feeling pretty good at the beginning of the conversation, they may pull you down a bit, but it is more likely that you will be able to raise their spirits and help them to feel better.

The more you can be around high-vibrational energy, the more it will benefit your own energy levels on a daily basis. And if you are constantly around high-vibrational people, then the impact can help to stimulate a long-term improvement in your own energies. You really are fundamentally affected by the company you keep.

Places also have a vibrational frequency to which we react. We all have places that we love and others that we find intimidating or uncomfortable. Some towns feel depressing and unwelcoming, whereas other towns feel upbeat and pleasant. Here, we are simply picking up on the collective vibrational frequency of the people who live in a particular place.

Changing energy frequency levels

As we progress through our life, we may find that we achieve success in different things – perhaps our career takes off and we become very good at what we do. This increases and reinforces our good opinion of ourselves, giving us more confidence in our own ability and changing our personal thought patterns. This increase in positive thought patterns means that our personal energy frequency rises. A similar, negative, effect can occur if you have a run of bad luck. If you find the problems you encounter too much to cope with, they are likely to depress your vibrational level.

We all experience natural vibrational fluctuations on a daily basis as we encounter and have to cope with life's everyday events. We have probably all experienced the feeling of being down in the dumps, when our problems seem huge and we can't see a way around them. If we have an interrupted night's sleep and wake up on a rainy day to news of a traffic jam on our route to work on the local radio, it can make things feel even worse. But with a good night's sleep and a ray of sunshine when you open the curtains next morning, you feel a new surge of energy and yesterday's problems diminish. What is happening is that we are simply viewing the same situation from a different frequency level.

Anna's typical day

Let us imagine that during any given day we have 100,000 thoughts going through our mind. These thoughts are influenced by day-to-day activities – people we meet, situations we encounter, whether our favourite team wins or loses, news in the newspapers and so on. The thoughts we have may be high-vibrational or low-vibrational, and each one has an influence on the vibration rate of our personal energy field, speeding it up or slowing it down as we go about our daily activities. Let us take a look at a typical day to give you an idea of how it works.

8.00 a.m.
It's a bright spring morning, the sun is shining, and it feels great to be alive. As Anna throws back the curtains, the sun's rays cascade into the bedroom, illuminating everything in a golden glow. This is one of those days when

she feels on top of the world. The children are relaxed and happy as they get ready for school. Anna's thoughts are **high-vibrational** and she feels content. Her mind is untouched by any of the **low-vibrational** situations that we all encounter every day. At this point of the day, it's fair to assume that her personal energy field is vibrating at a fairly fast rate.

8.30 a.m.

This is a great start, but – hang on – little Lucy is lagging behind and holding everybody up. 'Come on, Lucy. Hurry up or you will be late for school,' shouts Anna. A slight feeling of frustration sweeps over her. This is a **low-vibrational** emotion, and it slows Anna's personal energy field down slightly.

9.00 a.m.

'But it's still a great day,' Anna thinks to herself as she ushers the children into the car and sets off for school. A few jokes on the way ensure a happy and laughter-filled journey so, as this is a **high-vibrational** situation, it speeds up her personal energy field.

9.30 a.m.

The children are safely in school when up strolls Mrs Johnson. 'Oh, no!' Anna says to herself, 'who is she going to be gossiping about today?' Sure enough, away she goes: 'Well I don't know who she thinks she is …' and 'What they need a big car like that for I don't know …'. Now Anna's personal energy field is slowing down as she lends a sympathetic ear to Mrs Johnson and listens to her jealousy, resentment and envy directed at one person after another. The **low-vibrational** conversation is dragging down Anna's energy field. After 15 minutes, Mrs Johnson announces that she has to go, leaving Anna slightly dazed and feeling decidedly grumpy.

Anna's vibrational level is lowered by contact with another person's negative energy.

l0.00 a.m.

The journey home is uneventful; a good thing really, because Anna is in no mood for any aggravating drivers. After parking the car, she opens the front door to find a pile of letters waiting for her on the carpet. 'Let's see what we've got here then,' she thinks to herself. 'Gas bill, electricity bill, telephone bill, credit card bill and a couple of junk mail letters. Well, there shouldn't be too much to worry about there.' She decides to make a cup of tea before opening the mail.

First, the gas bill: it's slightly more than she was expecting, but their budget can cope with it. 'I wonder if we have a gas leak? No, we probably left the heating on more than I realised,' she thinks to herself. Suddenly **low-vibrational** thoughts begin to creep into her mind, and she starts to worry, so slowing down her personal energy field.

Next, the electricity bill. That's a lot lower than she expected, which is a nice bonus that makes up for the gas bill. She feels a little uplift, and a small wave of **high-vibrational** joy sweeps through her mind. Up goes her personal energy field.

Next, the credit card statement: not so bad!

But then she opens the telephone bill: £500! 'My goodness, how can that be?' Anxiety takes hold as she scrambles around for the itemised statement. 'I knew it! The Internet! I'll swing for him when he gets home!' A flood of **low-vibrational** emotions hit: worry, fear, anger. Anna's personal energy field plummets as she engages in this **low-vibrational** energy. By now, her personal energy field is slowing right down and she feels terrible. That's all she needed; now she has a headache as well.

11.00 a.m.

Anna spends the rest of the morning fretting over her financial problems and feeling very low indeed. 'Will anything ever go right?' she wonders? Suddenly her **low-vibrational** state is interrupted by the doorbell. As she opens the door, Anna is greeted by a big smile from Jane, her next door neighbour. 'Put the kettle on,' says Jane as she charges by, brimming with confidence and **high-vibrational** energy. 'You look fed up,' she says, catching Anna's miserable face. 'What's wrong?' Well, that's just what Anna needed, and she begins to pour out all her problems. As she fires each one towards Jane, Jane just bats it away with her usual **high-vibrational**, positive outlook. After an hour's conversation, Anna feels decidedly better. Jane has put her problems in perspective, and Anna's personal energy field has shot up. The **low-vibrational** thoughts that weighed heavily on her mind an hour ago now seem trivial, and strangely enough her headache has gone as well. Jane dashes off to her mother's, and Anna decides it's time to do the shopping.

Anna's vibrational level is raised by contact with another person's positive energy.

12.00 noon

The sun is bright (although Anna had failed to notice it during her **low-vibrational** morning). She soon has the car backed out of the drive and is heading towards town. She pulls into the car park. Everything seems rosy again, and her stressful morning feels like a distant memory. Her first stop is the butchers; she joins the queue and waits to be served. The butcher is always very friendly. As soon as he sees Anna, he remarks that she looks younger every time he sees her. Anna feels herself blush, but she is very pleased to receive the compliment and feels uplifted. The **high-vibrational** energy directed towards her has pushed up the frequency of her personal energy field, which also has the effect of making her feel good about herself: more **high-vibrational** thoughts, which drown out any **low-vibrational** thought patterns she normally carries about herself.

12.30 p.m.

Soon the shopping is done, and Anna heads back to the car park, laden down with bags. As she approaches the car, she hears a loud screeching noise heading towards her. She turns to see a car hurtling by at speed. It narrowly misses her, but she drops one of her bags of shopping – eggs, tins and fruit fall everywhere. Anna's heart is pounding at the thought of how close the car came to knocking her down – and not so much as an apology. Her initial feelings are fear and panic, but they are soon followed by frustration and anger. She is fuming! 'How could that idiot drive like that?' she thinks to herself. 'What if the children had been with me?' She decides to report the incident to the police. By this time her personal energy field has plummeted as a result of all this **low-vibrational** energy.

Anna's vibrational level plummets as a result of stress and anger.

2.30 p.m.

After two hours in the police station, Anna is feeling very fed up. The possibility of anything being done about the incident appears to be nil. Anna trudges out. Her personal energy field is now very slow indeed. To compound the situation, she is running late to pick up the children, so she dashes to the school, feeling decidedly down in the dumps. The children are very well behaved on the journey home, as they immediately sense Anna's bad mood. Once in the house, she chases them upstairs to do their homework while she makes the tea, her mind racing with the day's events. Bills, Mrs Johnson's gossiping, the car park incident ... Anna wallows in **low-vibrational** thoughts. Her personal energy field is slowing down even further. She feels really depressed. 'Why is life so stressful?' and 'Nothing seems to go right' are the kind of thoughts racing around in her head. The children avoid her, as they can see her bad mood has not lifted. Indeed, Anna's mind is pulsating with anger, which she is ready to direct at her husband when he gets home.

Anna prepares to direct her low-vibrational mood towards her husband.

5.00 p.m.
'Hello, darling!' shouts John, as he opens the front door. Anna is ready for him, fired up and angry. As she turns to face him, her mind is racing with what she is going to say, but he stops her dead in her tracks. 'For you,' he says, handing her a dozen red roses. 'I've booked a table at our favourite restaurant to celebrate my promotion! From now on it's only the best for us. My salary has gone up 20 per cent and they've thrown in a company car. Now, what is it you wanted to say?' All of a sudden Anna's anger and fear vanish; the good news from her husband has dissipated her

negativity. Suddenly, she is feeling good, and her personal energy field races up. 'It was nothing really,' she blurts out. 'Anyway, let's celebrate! What marvellous news!' The children come running down the stairs – they sense that the atmosphere has changed from **low-vibrational** to **high-vibrational** energy. Suddenly, the house is filled with happiness; Anna's bad day seems like a distant nightmare. How on earth had she allowed herself to get so down?

7.00 p.m.
A short while later, as she lies soaking in a hot bubble bath with a wonderful night in front of her, Anna thinks back over her day and begins to recognise how she became the victim of her own thinking. Every time she allowed a thought to grab hold of her and control her without offering any resistance, she became the victim of all the **low-vibrational** energy that had come her way. But, she realises, she did not have to engage with these **low-vibrational** energies quite so eagerly. If she could have detached herself from them, her personal energy field would not have been quite so affected. She didn't have to take it so much to heart when Mrs Johnson started resenting and envying everybody. She didn't have to let the bills get her down – she and John had always managed to get by. She didn't need to let the feelings of fear, panic, anger and frustration overwhelm her when the car screeched past her in the car park. And she didn't need to mull over all of these **low-vibrational incidents** for the rest of the afternoon, thus slowing down her personal energy field even further.

Anna's energy field

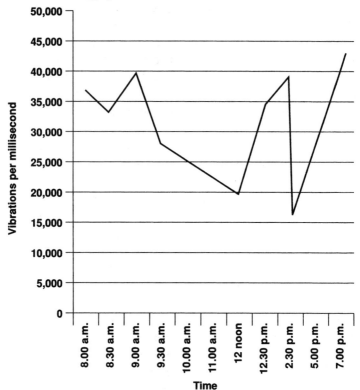

Fluctuations in Anna's energy field throughout the day.

As you can see from the graph, Anna's personal energy field has fluctuated throughout the day as she alternated between positive and negative thoughts – from a low point of 17,000 vibrations per millisecond at 2.30 p.m., when she had just left the police station, to a high point of 48,000 vibrations per millisecond at 7 p.m., as she lay in a hot bath with only positive thoughts in her mind. Remember, the faster our personal energy field vibrates, the better we feel, because we are closer to the high-vibrational energy of love.

Coping with negative energy

It doesn't matter what is pulling you down – the gas bill, the TV breaking down, the children stressing you out. You cannot avoid the low-vibrational energy in your environment; this is the very nature of life. What does matter is how you choose to react to these low-frequency attacks, because you can have some control over how much these situations and events affect you.

I recall an incident in my office in which one of the administrators had had a particularly stressful morning dealing with complaints of various sorts. This low-frequency energy had given her a headache. Then the telephone rang and she found out that she had just won quite a large amount of money. She happily passed on the story of her good fortune to the rest of the staff. A little later, I asked her if she still had a headache. To her amazement, she replied that it had completely disappeared. You see, sometimes even headaches can be instantly cured if you can find a way to lift your personal energy vibration.

On another occasion, a boy I know called Jordan lost his brand-new mobile phone. He was distraught, as his father had just bought him this expensive present. When he realised that he had lost his phone, his whole day looked completely different: one minute he was happy and enjoying himself and the next he was inconsolable. His mind had suddenly become filled with low-vibrational emotions: worry, fear, anger, frustration, disappointment. This had the effect of pulling down his energy frequency. It was several days before Jordan recovered and moved back up to his normal frequency level. That's how powerful negative energy can be.

If negative energy is so powerful, you need an equally powerful weapon to use against it – and that's high-vibrational thinking.

Taking Control

So let's briefly recap. Energy is vibrating all around us. The energy of love is high-vibrational; the energy of fear is low-vibrational. The closer we can stay to the vibration that we call love, the better we will succeed in all aspects of our lives.

Most of life's problems exist at the lower frequency levels, so if you are focused on low-vibrational energy, you are likely to be ill more often, end up in more arguments, have more trouble with your car or your computer, find it harder to get a job or succeed at work, and experience problems at school or with the children. In fact, everything will be much more difficult.

High-vibrational thinking is a way of learning to dismiss low-vibrational thoughts and replace them with high-vibrational thoughts. It makes absolute sense to try to think in a more high-vibrational way, because this puts you in control. And being able to control your thoughts and feelings will help you to change your life. You can learn to use high-vibrational thinking in every aspect of your life. You deserve the positive energies of love, happiness and joy in your life just as much as anyone else.

Just being aware of high-vibrational thinking is the first step to taking control of your energy field, as it enables you to understand what is happening in your mind and to appreciate that control is lacking. Once you have taken that first step, it won't be long before you automatically begin to assess situations in terms of energy and put HVT into practice without thinking about it. This makes a welcome change from being controlled by negative energies, tossed around like a rag doll in the wind.

Reprogramming our subconscious

There are two elements in making HVT work for you: one deals with your fundamental energy levels, and the other deals with how you react to the changing energy levels around you.

The influences we experience during our formative years help to establish our normal vibrational frequency and define our comfort zone: our fundamental feelings about ourselves and the kind of life we believe we deserve. Throughout our life, our subconscious mind monitors our feelings and actions so that we stay within the boundaries of our comfort zone – whether that is good for us or not. If we try to move away from that comfort zone, we are engaging in a battle for control – and it's a battle that we usually lose.

There is another way – one that avoids the battle and enables us to take control. The answer is to re-programme your subconscious mind and so change the boundaries of your comfort zone.

Let's take the dieting example that we looked at on pages 28–9. While your comfort zone is chips, chips and more chips, any diet will be a huge struggle that is almost doomed to failure, because you will be constantly drawn back to your comfort zone. But if you change the boundaries of your comfort zone, your subconscious mind will monitor what you eat to keep you at the newly programmed weight that is now within your comfort zone. You will be able to change your eating habits, with the result that you are attracted to a more healthy diet of less fattening foods. If you look at those people who have dieted successfully and lost lots of weight permanently, you will generally find that they have also successfully re-programmed their subconscious mind.

If it's improved fitness you are trying to achieve, the principles are just the same. While your comfort zone is an evening with your feet up in front of the TV, that is what your subconscious will be pulling you towards.

HVT is a way of re-programming that does away with the need for an iron will. This book will show you how to achieve that re-programming. The first step towards change is to understand how your mind works and accept the power of the subconscious mind. Once you appreciate this, you can begin to move forward and make plans for a new and exciting future.

With HVT you can re-train your inner child.

Of course, once you have re-programmed your subconscious into a new comfort zone, it will start to form new and more positive habits. If you have an established habit of taking regular exercise, when you miss your exercise for some reason, you will feel tired and drained. It's almost as if you are addicted to exercise and without it you feel down. This, again, is your subconscious pushing you to stick to the comfort zone – but in this case, of course, the comfort zone is healthy, so the subconscious is a force for good.

So you can see that your subconscious can be programmed for success or failure, and it will use all its powerful influence to maintain whatever it is programmed for. If we can re-programme our subconscious for success, clearly this is the answer to many of our problems. This book will show you how to do just that – to change your subconscious comfort zone in relation to the specific problems and issues that are relevant to you.

Start changing now

You don't have to wait until you have read the whole book to make changes in your life. You can start making changes straightaway. Start by dealing with the energy fluctuations you encounter on a daily basis and how you react to them.

Remember the outline of Anna's fairly ordinary day (see pages 40–7). Look at it again and you will see how Anna allowed herself to be engaged by the energies around her rather than taking control of her own energy field. When she encountered low-vibrational energy from outside, or when her own emotions were low-vibrational – both things we can't always avoid – she allowed herself to be dragged down and ended up feeling even worse. You are probably just the same. Now that you realise that by engaging with low-vibrational thoughts you are only going to damage yourself by dragging down your personal energy field, you can start to implement changes that will make an immediate difference to your life.

Don't engage with low-vibrational energy

The crucial thing is not to engage emotionally with low-vibrational energy, because it is when you become emotionally attached to negativity that you are most damaged. Your personal energy frequency will plummet and move you into a much more difficult frequency zone.

You can now recognise low-vibrational energy as anything that pulls you down and makes you feel negative: anger, disappointment, envy, spite and so on. When you encounter that kind of energy, the secret is to remain calm and to let the negative energy pass over you without buying into it. Try to visualise the energy moving away from you and disappearing, rather than hanging on to it and engaging with it mentally. The principle is very simple: recognise it and reject it.

Start right now. The next time you find low-vibrational thoughts coming into your mind, let them go. You almost certainly won't succeed straightaway; it will take a little practice, but even the first time you try it, you will feel some impact. Then, every time you succeed, it will become easier and more automatic to reject negativity. If you stick at it and follow the specific guidance in this book, you will get better at it every day.

Take bills as an example. If you have a gas bill that is higher than you expected, you obviously have to do something about it. But worrying is not going to make the bill any smaller; nor is it going to get it paid. If you put aside the worry, you have more energy to think about positive things that will help you to solve the actual problem of paying the bill. Your mind will be able to focus on the options: you can dip into your savings, contact the supplier and arrange to pay it off gradually, turn down the heating thermostat so it doesn't happen again – or whatever.

Concentrate on the present

So visualising negative energy draining away will help. Another very simple way to handle low-vibrational thought patterns is to concentrate on the present.

We all spend too much of our time thinking about the past or the future. Our minds tend to dwell on something that has happened or something that might happen until this becomes a habit that is difficult to break. In fact, we are often scarcely aware that we are doing this.

It is all too easy to dwell on a low-vibrational event that has happened in the past: the time we struggled to meet a payment date; the time someone shouted at us or let us down. We keep running it over and over again in our minds like some kind of loop-tape action replay. The result of replaying thoughts of anger, frustration, disappointment, fear or uncertainty is that our personal frequency level is dragged down even more, pulling us down into a negative zone.

Likewise, we may focus our attention on a future negative event that may never happen: the cold we are sure we are going to catch, the redundancy that is bound to come, and so on. Similarly, the effect is to lower our frequency level, leeching away all our positive energy.

The past is gone and we cannot change it. Dwelling on its negative energies will only drag us down. We simply need to learn from it and move on. The future is not here yet; worrying about something that may or may not happen will only drag down your personal energy field, making life much harder in the process.

If you can avoid this time trap and think in the present, you will find that your energy levels remain high. By being alert to this pitfall, you can train your mind to recognise when you are about to fall into the trap. Then you simply stop and remind yourself to concentrate on the present. If you have a problem, look at what you can do now to solve it in the best possible way.

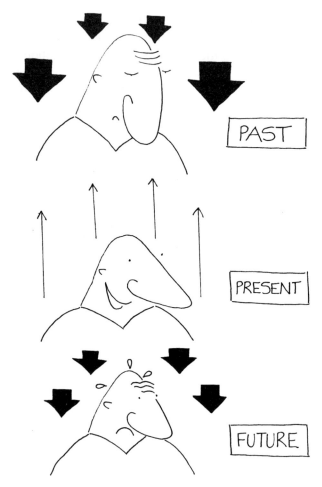

Dwelling on the past and worrying about the future is a waste of energy. Stay focused in the present if you want to get the best out of your life.

Use high-vibrational thinking to clear your mind of clutter and stay focused in the present moment; then you are ready to handle life to the best of your ability.

Take one step at a time
There will be times when you don't manage to dismiss low-vibrational thoughts altogether. Don't worry about it – for worrying is in itself hanging on to low-vibrational energies. Look at what you did achieve; tell yourself how much better you did it than last time; congratulate yourself and move on. Before long you will find that you are more and more in control. This means that your personal energy field will not slow down as easily next time you encounter low-vibrational energy, and you won't have to spend every day on a mental rollercoaster ride.

Remember, you are more in control than you realise. Your thoughts create your reality, so if you fill your mind with high-vibrational thoughts, you will have a more positive, enjoyable and fulfilling life. You can take control of your own energy.

How Does Bullying Start?

As you now know, we all have our own natural energy frequency, and the actions and emotions of other people impact on our energy level.

A person who becomes a bully is someone whose energy field is generally vibrating at a low frequency. Whatever the reason for these low-vibrational thought patterns, the result is the same: the person feels unlovable and not deserving of love, which means that they constantly monitor their energy frequency levels to make sure that they stay low. They may well have negative thoughts such as: 'I am ugly', 'I am stupid', 'I am

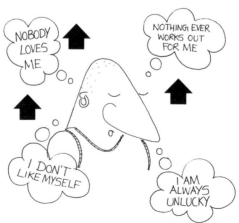

A bully has a low opinion of himself.

unlucky', 'nothing ever works out for me', 'I can't do anything'. These types of powerful low-vibrational affirmations ensure that their frequency levels are kept down.

Of course, not everyone who fits this description turns into a bully. What distinguishes a bully is that they attempt to damage other people in order to make themselves feel better, although they may not even realise that they are engaged in this negative behaviour pattern. In fact, it is more than likely that they have been bullied themselves at some time in their lives and that this is, at least in part, responsible for their dislike of themselves and their feeling that they are not worth much. However, they recognise subconsciously that the behaviour of the bully towards them made that person feel better at their expense, and therefore see bullying as a way of making themselves feel better too.

Bullies are really weak and insecure people who dislike themselves.

Bullying often starts with boasting

Initially, bullies often try to improve their self-esteem by boasting. Through bragging about themselves they hope to gain the respect and admiration of others. When this kind of high-vibrational energy is directed towards the bully, it has the effect of temporarily raising their energy frequency, making them feel good. This gives them a short-term lift and makes them feel better about themselves. Boasting may also make other people look up to the bully. I have myself witnessed people lying about their position at work in order to impress others – and becoming so involved in the pretence that they develop more and more fabricated stories about their role.

The problem is that boasting creates a negative energy, as it is, at best, based on exaggeration and the attempt to force respect rather than earning it. At worst, it is just a tissue of lies. Because the potential bully is not in reality positive, successful or important – as they are making themselves out to be – any admirers soon see through them. The admiration, and the good feeling it engenders, therefore quickly disappears.

Being found out

Once the truth behind the bully's boasting has been found out – and it always is – the bully's own negative feelings about themselves are confirmed. The whole complex of negative thought patterns that is buried deep within their subconscious is activated. These are their own personal insecurities about themselves, which are usually kept just below the surface but are always ready to emerge if given the opportunity. They are low-vibrational thoughts and feelings, such as inadequacy, self-doubt and the belief that they don't deserve love in their lives.

In addition, the bully now has to deal with even more negative energies directed at them from outside as a result of the discovery that they are not who they pretended to be: disbelief, scorn, even contempt.

The start of bullying

Being caught out and realising that people see them for the person that they really are can be devastating to the bully. It makes for a situation that is very hard for them to deal with. They need to find another way to feel better, and so they turn all their bad feelings about themselves on to another person, holding that person responsible for all their problems.

They may turn their negativity on the person who has found them out and become very aggressive towards them. But if this person is strong and self-assured, this will not be possible. In that case, the bully may find it impossible to look this person in the eye; they will not be able stand being around them (because they know the bully for what they really are they), and they may even leave their job or move away to avoid this unbearable confrontation.

If they cannot intimidate the person who found them out, the bully will usually put themselves into another environment and look for someone else to blame, someone vulnerable who they can victimise. They select a target and direct all their low-vibrational energy towards that target in order to make themselves feel better. This may take the form of violence, but more often it will manifest as a constant barrage of insults and subtle negative comments. The effect of this attack is to lower the victim's vibrational frequency, making them feel worse about themselves, while raising the bully's vibrational frequency. The bully will show no concern for the person they are hurting, because their real focus is wholly on themselves.

The bully will usually try to turn everybody else against their target as well, and will use any means possible to achieve this. They will point out the target's

Bullies like to make you feel bad about yourself; this pulls down your energy frequency and makes them feel temporarily better about themselves.

failings, insult them openly and start up negative gossip – each time trying to make themselves feel better. Gathering support helps the bully to justify their selfish, hurtful behaviour and also gives them an added feeling of control and power. This pushes up their energy frequency and gives them another short-term high.

The vicious circle

Because the bully's 'high' is not founded on any real positive feelings about themselves, it is short-lived, so they have to start being mean to someone all over again. If they keep picking on the same person, they will chip away at the victim's self-esteem, making it easier every time to score points against them.

Each time they make an unkind or vicious comment, the bully feels better, but each time the good feeling disappears more quickly. So they lock themselves into a vicious circle of ever-diminishing returns.

The bully will often keep up the vendetta until the victim cannot stand it any more and leaves. However, if the victim can hang on in there and find a way to deal with the bullying, eventually the bully will almost certainly be the one to leave – as in the end they will simply stop deriving any kind of 'high' from the bullying.

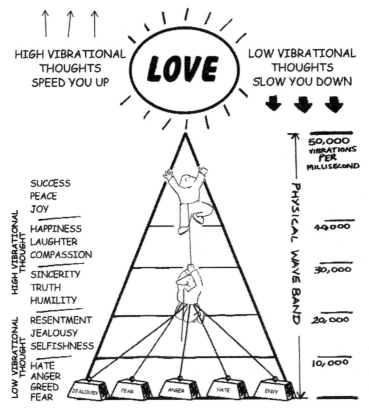

Bullies are held down by low-vibrational thought patterns such as hate and jealousy; as a result, they try to pull someone else down to their level.

Damage to the environment

All this negative behaviour is damaging not only to the people directly concerned but also to the others in the place where it is happening. Bullying colours the environment with low-vibrational energy and creates a general sense of bad feeling.

I have witnessed how destructive this can be. Indeed, I have seen one person almost bring down a business because of this damaging behaviour. It is very easy for the situation to get out of hand, as gradually everyone becomes caught up in the storm of negativity and suffers the consequences. The low-frequency situation tends to drag down everybody's vibrational level into a zone of poor productivity, arguments and strained working relationships. This can happen in any group situation – a business, a school, a football team – and, unfortunately, it is happening in most places to some degree.

Keeping out of this kind of low-frequency mayhem is easier said than done; you can be drawn into it without even realising that it has happened. However, once you have mastered HVT, you will be able to see when this is taking place and have some control over its effect on you.

Why Do They Pick on Me?

It is important to identify what makes one person more of a potential target for a bully than another, because this helps us to understand what is going on when bullying happens – and how to change it.

It's no coincidence that strong, confident and successful people don't usually become the target for bullies. This is because, as we have said, bullies are weak people themselves (even though they like to portray themselves as tough), so they always pick on somebody who appears weaker – either physically or emotionally – than they are. The last thing they expect, or want, is for somebody to stand up to them, so obviously they are going to target where there is most chance of the victim caving in.

If a bully notices that a person is sensitive about a particular thing, they may pick on them, seizing that issue as their target. Alternatively, they may choose someone who would rather put up with abusive treatment than risk offending the bully. Bullies are also often motivated by resentment and envy, selecting as a target someone who possesses qualities that they lack and then focusing on those qualities and making fun of them.

Low-vibrational energy

A bully knows if they can frighten and intimidate a person, and if they can, this is exactly what they will do. What you need to remember if you are the victim is that they are consumed with low-vibrational energy (negative thoughts about themselves) and are trying to drag you down to their level by attacking you in whatever way they think will be most effective.

But you don't have to put up with this. You can stop the bully. You are not weaker than they are; you can be stronger. In this book I am going to show you how to find your strength so that you can change what is happening.

Where Bullying Happens and What Happens as a Result

Bullying can – and unfortunately does – happen anywhere and to anyone. Bullies exist in every area of life; they may be work colleagues, your best friend, your spouse or even your parents. They come in all shapes and sizes, and can be men, women or children.

Bullies come in all shapes and sizes and could be anybody in your life.

Often we are very clear that we are in a situation where bullying is happening to us or to someone we know, but this is not always the case. Sometimes we fail to recognise bullying as such. In this section we are going to look at a few examples of bullying so that you can see the different ways in which it can present itself. The common factor in all of these examples is that someone is trying to make themselves feel better by putting someone else down.

Persistent negative comments, snide remarks and relatively minor physical intimidation – let alone full-blown physical attacks – can have a devastating effect when repeated over a period of time. The more often these things occur, the lower your energy levels become and the more permanent this negative state will be. Don't think that just because someone is only poking you or making fun of your haircut it is not serious and you should not be affected by it. Drips of water will wear away a stone if the water goes on dripping for long enough. The first step in the healing process is to admit that this is making you feel bad. And, yes, you can do something to stop it.

How bullying can make you feel

If you are being bullied, you may begin to feel low and depressed, even tearful. You may start to dread going to school or work, and you may lose your confidence in your own abilities in all kinds of areas. The more fearful you feel, the more deeply and thoroughly your life will be affected. Bullying can bring all your deep-rooted insecurities to the surface, and this can have a devastating effect on your personal energy frequency. Exactly how you react will depend on your own personality and circumstances, but whatever the reaction, it will be related to low-vibrational feelings at the bottom of the scale.

Bullies can be friends

Bullying is common among acquaintances and so-called friends. I have witnessed this first-hand on many occasions. There are in fact instances where someone a person considers to be their best friend is actually doing them a great deal of harm.

Bullying 'friends' are likely to appear to be very protective of you. They may keep reminding you that you are their best friend and will place great importance on your friendship, constantly reminding you of their affection for you and sometimes even referring to you as being like a brother or sister. They may like to copy you and often declare how much the two of you are alike.

They may also try to keep you away from anyone who distracts your attention from them and will put down other people who they feel are getting too close to you or threatening their control over you. They will have no hesitation in turning you against such people. Indeed, they will think nothing of destroying your relationships with other people and feel no remorse if they can achieve this. Lying – or at least distorting the truth – to achieve their objective will not be beyond them.

Such friends may show little interest in your problems but will frequently use you as a listening post for their own, expecting you to sympathise over all their moans and groans. They will not take no for an answer and will be most put out if you ever have to let them down, although they'll have no hesitation in letting you down without a second thought and will expect you to accept that without question.

They will drop you like a brick when it suits them but expect you to be there for them whenever they want you. If you challenge their behaviour, they will turn against you and tell everyone how badly you have treated them, how you abused the friendship and just used them for your own ends.

The effect of bullying friends

Although you may initially be attracted by such a 'friend's' interest, their apparent love for you may very soon come to make you feel a little uncomfortable, bordering as it does on possessiveness and obsession. You may feel constrained in who you talk to and want to branch out and be friendly with other people but feel you can't do that without offending them. This will make you feel even more uncomfortable in their company. You will probably always feel on edge with such a person, knowing that you must be careful not to upset or offend them.

Such people are very damaging, and if there is someone like this in your life, you need to identify and move away from them. They are out for themselves in a big way and are nobody's friend but their own. They will use you and hurt you to get what they want, which is to feel better about themselves on a daily basis. They perpetrate one of the worst forms of bullying, which often goes undetected, their sole aim being to increase their personal energy frequency at your expense at every opportunity.

Friends who pick on other people

Being with a person who constantly picks on other people can have a strongly negative impact on you, even though you are not the direct victim of the bully.

I remember a guy I used to meet fairly regularly for a meal. Whatever the meal or the restaurant was like, he always seemed to be able to find something to complain about. He seemed to feel that the act of complaining gave him power over the waiter, and the low-vibrational comments he made certainly pulled down the waiter's energy frequency. This had the desired effect of momentarily making my friend feel better about himself – but it didn't last long. So then he had to find another opportunity to bully somebody. Even when the meal was absolutely excellent, he would always manage to find something to be negative about, thus fulfilling his need to put somebody down.

Why is this bullying rather than just being miserable? The answer is because he did it so regularly and so frequently and because he was using his power as a customer to be nasty to someone else, knowing that they could not answer back.

This man was a bully because he had such a poor opinion of himself that pulling down somebody's energy frequency could make him feel better about himself for a few seconds by closing the gap between his vibrational rate and the waiter's. For this short while he believed he had power over someone, and this made him feel superior, giving him a temporary lift.

Obviously, this behaviour had an effect on the waiter, undermining his confidence in his professional ability and generally making him feel low. However, the behaviour also had a lowering effect on me because of all the negative energy circulating. After a while, I was able to take myself out of the situation because I could see this man for what he was, but if I had regularly been in his company it would have become very hard to resist the dragging effect of those negative energies. It is quite possible that I could have ended up becoming the butt of his bullying myself.

Bullying at work

Another bully I knew at one time seemed at first to be charming and articulate, but he used classic bullying techniques to try to increase his energy frequency. He was a supervisor in an office, so had a number of people working for him.

His first tactic was to try to impress me with stories about what he had and hadn't done, but it didn't take me long to realise that much – if not all – of what he said was complete fabrication. Once I got to know him and began to realise he was not quite the person I thought he was, his tactics changed. He became arrogant and conceited and used his position of power to try to dominate and talk down to me. This was very damaging to the company he was working for, as all he really achieved was upsetting and distancing his own staff, pulling down the energy frequency of the business in the process.

The boss who's a bully

It is, sadly, not uncommon for people at work to bully those who are in a subordinate position. They feel that because they have a degree of authority over someone else, they can use it to dominate and insult that person. This reduces general confidence, induces stress, and encourages a highly negative atmosphere in the workplace. No one can work well or give of their best if they feel not just undervalued but also insulted.

In fact, this behaviour is a complete misuse of power. A manager's true role is to encourage and guide the people in their department, helping them to be as happy and as productive in their job as possible.

Bullying at school

Bullying at school remains a major problem and one that we desperately need to find a solution to. School bullying is responsible for much unhappiness, and many children do not achieve their potential because of it. A child can be made so unhappy by bullying that they are unable to enjoy what should be some of the happiest years of their lives and instead spend their childhood in a low-frequency, depressed state.

If bullying involves small attacks, you might not even notice them at first. It's only when they have continued for some time that you start to realise their effect on you. That may be days, weeks or months, depending on your own character and the nature of the attacks.

How do bullies work at school? The classic bully uses constantly repeated insults to try to put other people down: 'You're useless at maths', 'My dad's richer than your dad', 'You don't have any friends, Johnny No-mates!' They use ridicule and attempt to get as many other people on their side as they can. They are often very observant and notice which insult stings the most, then use it over and over again.

They may also resort to violence, perhaps starting with a pinch, a kick or a pull of the hair. In isolation, each individual incident may not seem major, but collectively, they can be hugely damaging, wearing slowly away at the victim's self-esteem.

School bullies may also masquerade as the friend of their victim. They may make throw-away casual comments, for example about your appearance or your weight, that appear to be harmless remarks. This apparent harmlessness is part of the strategy: if you object, they can claim they were only joking and try to make you feel bad about taking a stand. By using this strategy, the bully can often appear to be charming and humorous when in fact they are conducting a calculated and deliberate attack.

The bully's ability to appear friendly often puts even more negative pressure on their victim. If the cycle is not broken, it can cause long-lasting damage to a child. Remember, though, that you can put a stop to it. Just reading this book is part of the process of strengthening your resolve so that you are ready to start acting to make things better for yourself.

The effect of bullying at school
School bullying has many repercussions as victims try and fail to cope. They may resort to truancy and bad

behaviour; their school work will almost certainly suffer; they may become lethargic or even depressed. The signs are not difficult for friends, parents and teachers to spot if they are observant and attentive to the well-being of the children in their care.

If you are a parent, look out for these indications that your child is being bullied. The sooner you can identify the problem, the sooner you can deal with it. If your child's normal frequency level is being dragged down by a bully, they may be behaving totally out of character. Avoid punishing them, as this behaviour is out of their control, due to the low-vibrational thoughts and feelings they are having about themselves as a result of bullying. (For more information, see the following chapter.)

Bullying and low-vibrational energies
All these negative feelings are the result of the bully directing their low-vibrational energy towards you. When someone directs energy of any kind at you, you have to cope with it. If it is low-vibrational energy, it is hard to combat and is likely to pull down your own energy levels – if you let it. This will in turn open the floodgates for low-vibrational thought patterns to flood your mind. And low-vibrational energy is bad for you!

Guidance for Parents

If you are parent who is reading this book because you are worried that your child is, or may be, being bullied, you may already have recognised some of the signs I have mentioned. If not, it is important that you watch out for any tell-tale indications that bullying is taking place.

If your child is being bullied, and their energy frequency therefore pulled down into a lower zone, this will result in different behaviour patterns. For example, they may well be naughtier with you than usual. If they feel they have no power at school, they may try to exercise power over you – even if it is only by refusing to go to bed on time or do their homework. So if your child is misbehaving or acting unusually, try to look a little deeper for the cause of this negativity. This kind of behaviour does not necessarily indicate bullying, but it is a possibility.

You will know from your own experience that when your energy frequency is lowered, you feel totally different about the world around you. Compare the feeling of getting up for a difficult meeting at work on a rainy Monday morning with sitting in the garden in the summer sunshine with a group of friends and a bottle of good wine! Even when you know what is happening, it can be tremendously difficult to pull out of a low-energy state. Imagine how hard it is for your child if they don't understand what is going on.

What to look out for

All responsible parents keep a watchful eye over their children and will notice if they are behaving out of character. The following are signs that bullying may be a problem:

▸ The child is unusually quiet and subdued.
▸ The child is lacking in energy.
▸ The child is unmotivated.
▸ The child seems to find it difficult to concentrate; even their favourite television programmes may not be able to hold their attention.
▸ The child often appears to be daydreaming, in a world of their own.
▸ The child spends more time than usual in their bedroom, away from the rest of the family.
▸ The child has gone off their food, not eating as much as normal.
▸ The child has become short-tempered and prone to angry outbursts.
▸ The child appears over-sensitive and emotional.
▸ The child doesn't want to go out of the house and play with their friends.
▸ The child has started to be aggressive towards their friends.
▸ The child's schoolwork is suffering.
▸ The child's general behaviour is deteriorating.
▸ The child shows a lack of respect for others.
▸ The child has become withdrawn and not very talkative.
▸ The child has become untidy in both their personal appearance and in general.
▸ The child is playing truant from school.
▸ The child is complaining of feeling ill.

- ▸ The child is behaving unusually, for example stealing or damaging things.
- ▸ The child puts themselves down.
- ▸ The child has more tantrums or displays of defiance than usual.
- ▸ The child is resorting to self-harm.

All of the above are signs that your child is in the low frequency zone that encourages dysfunctional behaviour. Of course, many children find themselves in this zone for reasons other than bullying; however – particularly if your child has suddenly started demonstrating low-frequency behaviour – consider bullying as a possible cause.

The longer your child's frequency zone is depressed by the attentions of a bully, the greater the chance of long-term damage, in which they come to believe in the low self-image that has been foisted on them by the bully. Eventually, indeed, their subconscious mind may begin to see this level of self-esteem as their new comfort zone and start to work to keep them there. This is how more bullies are created, as bullied children in this long-term depressed state often attempt to deal with their negative beliefs about themselves by bullying another child. Such behaviour is seldom motivated by an actual desire to hurt somebody.

Take action

The first thing to do is to try to find out what is happening. Talk to your child. It is more than likely that initially they will be defensive, and you will need all your patience and understanding, but persevere. The sooner the situation is tackled, the sooner it will begin to improve.

Talk to your child's teachers, but without making a big issue of the situation – this will only make it worse for your child. Be sensitive to their situation and don't storm into the classroom pointing your finger! That won't help.

Explain to your child what you think is going on and tell them in simple language about energy levels and how they affect people. Introduce them to HVT. Don't expect a reaction too early on, but as long as they are listening, you will be making a start in helping them. Remember, too, that your child needs love and affection more than ever in order to pull out of the low-frequency zone.

Read up on all the techniques in this book and gradually suggest strategies that will help your child to overcome their problems. It will take time and patience, so go slowly. You can help to turn the situation around.

Techniques to Break the Cycle

I believe that HVT offers a new perspective on bullying and a positive solution to the problem. Educating everybody involved about how the bullying process works and empowering them by introducing them to HVT are huge steps towards finding an answer to this very serious problem.

Remember that bullying occurs for only one reason: to enable the bully to feel better about themselves. They do this by trying to pull down your energy frequency. HVT shows bullies up for what they really are, and once you have learnt to use it, you will have the ability to identify bullies and stop them having a negative effect on you, giving you control over the situation. Indeed, with the help of HVT you will eventually be able to root bullies out of your life once and for all.

The first affirmation
The first step in dealing with bullying is to affirm to yourself that you are going to change your life. You can and will do so if you persevere. Keep reminding yourself that you are going to cope with this bullying once and for all and will not attract it into your life again. Write your affirmation down on a piece of paper and stick it on the fridge door or keep it in your pocket – write it on the back of your hand if you like. Keep reminding yourself of your affirmation all the time.

Spot the bully and avoid them

The next step is to be able to identify bullying when it enters your life. So how do you spot a bully?

Serial bullies are unhappy with themselves and cannot bear to spend too much time on their own, so they tend to go around in like-minded groups and look for people to feed off. Spending time on their own means they have to look into themselves, where they are likely to find only negative thoughts, so they close themselves off from thinking about themselves and are never self-aware. Look out for people who are never on their own and tend to be aggressive – not necessarily physically but perhaps verbally – with other people.

Watch out for anybody who makes you feel drained when you are with them; this is someone sapping your personal energy. People we enjoy being with make us feel good about ourselves. If someone you are spending time with makes you start to question your own abilities or lose your self-confidence, it's a bad sign. Be very wary of so-called friends who drain your energy or make you feel depressed or lethargic.

Bullies are often able to get you doing things or going places that you don't really want anything to do with. If a 'friendship' is very one-sided, it may not be good for you. In any friendship, there should be give and take.

If you think there is a bully in your life, what can you do about it? As far as possible, try to avoid the bully. Start to make your own plans, talk to other people and make arrangements to meet with them. You will find that their high-vibrational energy will help you to build up your own energy levels. It may be difficult to begin with, so start with small plans that will be effective but not too noticeable to the bully. For example, as you come out of class, say, 'I must rush to the loo before the next lesson' if that helps you to avoid sitting next to someone you don't want to. Each time you score a small victory, it will increase your confidence, raise your energy levels and help you to cope even better next time.

It's not your problem

Always remember that the bully is the person with the problem, not you. You don't need to let them draw you into their affairs; concentrate on yourself and making things better for you.

You now know that the bully is likely to have a low opinion of themselves and that this keeps their energy frequency vibrating at a slow rate. They may well have been bullied themselves, so they, too, may be a victim and need help to understand what is happening to them. They may be unaware of the fact that they are bullying other people because they are simply following a pattern established as the norm in their own life. They may not actually be trying to hurt you so much as following through a daily process that is focused on their own survival in terms of their ability to live with themselves.

When you no longer react to a bully, they are likely to move on and find somebody else who will. So they continue to promote negativity elsewhere. This is why, ultimately, the bully also needs to understand the bullying process so that they can stop being a slave to the negative patterns that rule their lives.

You may even be able to help the bully at some stage, but you should not worry about that now. Use the information in this book to empower yourself to improve your own situation. You are the most important person now, so take strength from your increased knowledge of how vibrational energy works and use it to heal yourself.

As I have already mentioned, the first step on the road to stopping bullying is recognising what is happening. By the time you have reached this stage in the book, you will already have taken this step. Now you are ready to start acting on your new-found knowledge.

Let comments pass you by

If you are subject to vicious comments, the next time the bully says something derogatory, recognise it for what it is (a mark of the bully's own insecurity), then try to let it pass you by. Don't think about it; certainly don't latch on to it and turn it over in your mind; don't believe it; don't engage emotionally with it. The bully's low-vibrational comments can only hurt you and pull down your frequency if you take them to heart, so just think to yourself, 'I know what you are doing and I am not affected by it.' They can only affect you if you let them.

Don't let a bully see that they are bothering you. If you get picked on, act as if it doesn't affect you. If a bully calls you names, ignore them and don't let yourself believe that there's any truth in what they are calling you – there isn't!

Try to imagine the comment as something physical – perhaps a tennis ball – that has been thrown at you but that you can easily step out of the way to avoid. Thus it bounces harmlessly behind you. You may find this difficult the first time you try, but keep at it and it will get easier every time. If a different image works better for you, then use that. You might see the comment as a custard pie that hits someone standing behind you. You might see it as a *Star Trek*-style laser stun-gun from which you are protected by an invisible energy shield so that the ray bounces harmlessly away from you. It's just imagination; anything goes!

Return to sender

Another very effective visualisation exercise is to imagine a huge mirror between you and the bully. Every time the bully attacks you, imagine that the low-vibrational energy is hitting the mirror and bouncing right back at them.

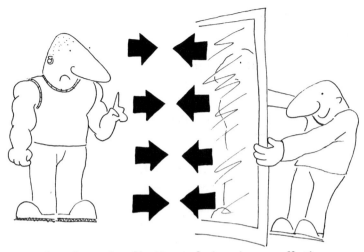

The mirror visualisation technique is very effective against bullying.

This visualisation has a double impact. Not only does the mirror protect you from the harmful low-vibrational energy but it also returns it to the bully, so they have to deal with it. The laser image works well here too – the bully has to endure the injury they were trying to inflict on you.

Stand up for yourself

Once you have started to use these techniques, you will soon find your energies increasing. Don't stop there! Keep on telling yourself that you are going to change for the better, and things will keep on getting better. The more you can avoid low-vibrational energy and be around people with high-vibrational energy, the easier it will be to generate high-vibrational energy of your own. Then you are really in charge!

You will find that you soon feel more confident in making a stand against any bullies you have identified in your life. You don't need to be aggressive; it's a case of being firm and decisive. Think in advance about what you are going to say. If you don't want to go somewhere with the bully, say something like, 'I'm really sorry but I can't go on that day. I've arranged to go out with (name a friend).' If they accuse you of being selfish or standing them up, tell them, 'No, I made the arrangement with (name of friend) last week. I don't want to let him/her down.' Then leave the situation.

When you have gained a little more confidence, start to speak up for yourself and don't be frightened to state your opinion. You have just as much right to your view as anyone else. Practise telling people what you think.

Stand tall and smarten up
It may be hard to believe, but you can use your physical stance and appearance to help you defeat bullies, too. Try an experiment. Think about the person who is bullying you, then go and slump in a corner, curling in on yourself. How does that make you feel? Now think of the bully again, but this time stand up tall, push your chin out and pull your shoulders back. Take a few deep breaths in and out. Feel better? I'm sure you do.

The next time you come across the bully, look them straight in the eye and stand tall. Breathe deeply. It will make a real difference.

Also think about your clothes and appearance. You don't have to be a fashion icon; just make sure your clothes are clean and tidy. Clean your fingernails, and wash and brush your hair. Look at yourself in the mirror and tell yourself how good you look. It's all about raising those energy levels, and small things like this will make a difference.

Turn the conversation on its head
Another useful technique is to practise changing the direction of a conversation. You can learn a lot about this

from politicians on the television! If the interviewer asks them a question they don't want to answer, they just start talking about something else. If a bully is draining you of your energy by pouring out all their problems, don't let them do it. Instead of just listening to their negativity, interrupt politely and start talking about something more positive. You may even raise their energy level and help them not to be so nasty! If not, they'll soon get fed up with not getting the response they want and will leave you alone.

Use the same tactic if a bully tries to turn you against other people. Stick up for that person if you feel strong enough. If you are not up to that just yet, simply stop the conversation and change the subject. You could say something like, 'Well, I don't think they're that bad … Do you fancy a cup of tea / a walk round the shops?' Again, the bully will soon tire of this treatment and seek out somebody who will listen to them. Bullies need you to engage in their negativity. If you do not do this, they will soon leave you alone.

Taking the Issue to the Comfort Zone

The tactics described in the previous chapter will help you to deal with the current bullying episode, but you also need to deal with the crucial issue of your own subconscious programming, which we looked at earlier (see How Our Emotional Frequency Is Established). You need to understand your own comfort zone and how you can make it work in your favour.

Just to recap, when you were young, your subconscious mind established a set of rules to govern what it sees as normal for you, and it is monitoring you to ensure that you stay within its boundaries. As a victim of bullying, the likelihood is that your subconscious is telling you that you can expect to be bullied, or that you don't deserve any better.

You may have been bossed around or bullied as a child by one of your family or friends and grown up to believe, on a subconscious level, that this is normal. It may not have been serious bullying; indeed, it could have been so subtle that you did not define it as such. However, your subconscious will have noticed this behaviour and regarded it as within your comfort zone, so now if you encounter someone who bullies you in a similar way, your subconscious will recognise this as normal and acceptable.

You will begin to absorb the negative, low-vibrational energies being directed at you by the bully rather than protecting yourself and sending them back.

The power of the subconscious

Let's look at an extreme example to clarify how this works. We have all heard tragic stories about women who have been bullied by their husbands but find it completely impossible to leave the relationship. Even if they do manage to get away, many go back, only to suffer the same fate again. Such women frequently feel that the situation is their fault, that they drove their husband to the attacks and that they actually deserve them. Even if such a woman manages to leave an abusive husband, she will frequently go on to embark on a similar relationship with another man.

This scenario demonstrates how powerfully our subconscious mind can programme our actions, and how it can keep us returning to our comfort zone. In this case, the women's subconscious is pushing them towards the same kind of man and making them feel attracted to him because that is what is in their programming.

Here's an example from my own experience, which I found very surprising but which clearly demonstrates how this process works. Not long ago, I had arranged to go for a night out with a friend of mine, and he brought along his brother. We had decided to go to a nearby town and tour a few bars. We had been there many times before and had always had quite a pleasant evening. When we told my friend's brother where we were going, he became very apprehensive and said he felt it was a rough area and he didn't want any trouble. I explained to him that we had been there many times before and never seen any trouble. This reassured him, and off we went.

As the night wore on, I noticed on at least five occasions my friend's brother attracting the attention of aggressive men who seemed to be staring at him for no apparent reason. We managed to stay out of trouble, but I was perturbed at the apparent bullying tactics of some of the people we came across. I was startled at the way they honed in on my friend's brother but not on me or my friend. With my friend's brother there, the place we were visiting seemed to be a rough and aggressive town, which it had never given the impression of being before. In fact, what I had glimpsed was my friend's brother's view of reality. He had expected this kind of bullying behaviour, and his expectations were fulfilled.

Your subconscious mind is so powerful that what it expects to happen in your life will more than likely happen. In this case, my friend's brother had expected to attract the attention of bullies, and his fear had made him a prime target. He had given off all the signals that a bully would be looking for – fear, apprehension, nervousness – and his behaviour attracted the bullies' attention. Because I was not giving off these signals, I was not even aware that the bullies where there until I noticed what was happening to my friend's brother.

If you recognise yourself in either of these examples, then you need to start re-programming your subconscious.

You are worth it!

Start by telling yourself you are worth just as much as anyone else – and keep on telling yourself. Write it down, post it on the wall, jot it down in your notebook. Don't miss any opportunity to tell yourself you are valuable. There's any number of ways you can do this, but specific examples of what is good about you often work best, as you will believe yourself when you use them. (If you get too carried away – 'I'm the most stunning creature ever to have walked the earth!' – you won't be able to believe your own affirmation, however hard you try.)

Try some of these ideas. Tell yourself:

▸ I have great hair.
▸ I'm a brilliant cook.
▸ I have a good figure.
▸ I'm fantastic at football.
▸ I presented an excellent report for work.
▸ My bum looks stunning in this!

Keep on at yourself all the time, remarking on every small success. You'll be surprised at how quickly they mount up and how much high-vibrational energy you'll generate each time you pay yourself a compliment.

Take it a step at a time

Next you can start tackling specific activities and changing habits. To begin with, view each one separately. Don't try to take on everything at once. For example, if you are going out for a drink with friends, spend half an hour before you go thinking about all the good things that could happen while you are out. You could go to a lively bar – if that's what you like – and chat to some interesting people. You could enjoy a few pints of your favourite beer. You could feel that you look good in your new shirt. You will be with friends who will help you have a good time. Brush away any negative thoughts. Again, you won't succeed completely the first time, but just trying will have a positive impact on your energy levels, and each time you do this exercise, it will feel better.

Let's take another example. Imagine that you are worried about someone bullying you in the playground. To raise your vibrational energy you might think about playing football with some other mates and scoring a goal, or eating a nice lunch with your favourite chocolate bar. Don't think about being on your own or being pestered by people you don't like. Think positive.

Re-evaluate yourself

Think about the kinds of things you want in your life and make a list of them. Don't go over the top; be realistic. But don't accept negative ideas either. Try to cover all aspects of your life. Once you have a list of, say, 20 things, type it out or write it out neatly and pin it somewhere where you can see it every day. If you don't want anyone else to see it, keep it under your pillow and look at it at night and in the morning. Here are a few ideas to get you started:

▶ I deserve a good job. I am going to be a mechanic.
▶ I am going to have a holiday in the sun every summer.
▶ I am a hard worker and I deserve to be promoted in five years' time.
▶ I have lots of friends who enjoy spending time with me.

Keep telling yourself all these good things and eventually your subconscious will get the message and move the boundaries of your comfort zone to a better and more rewarding position.

How Can I Help my Child?

All the techniques in the previous chapters work whether you are putting them into practice yourself or whether you are trying to help your child, but there are some additional things you can do to help younger children to understand what is going on and to reassure them that things will change. Remember that what you are trying to achieve here is to raise the frequency of your child's personal energy field to counteract the negative impact that bullying can have.

Your objective is to solidify the family home base, making your child feel as secure and important as possible. They need to feel loved and cared for in order to keep their personal energy frequency at higher levels and be able to deal with the negatives, such as bullying, that life may throw at them.

It is important, too, not to blame yourself if your child is being bullied. Children who already receive lots of love and attention from their parents can nevertheless become victims of bullies. In such cases, they will still need help to bring them back up from the lower-frequency zone that they have been dragged down into. And, of course, giving your child extra love and attention will never do any harm; it can only be beneficial.

Family time

Increase family time together, centred on the child's interests, to promote a feeling of love and security. This will affirm the child's position within the family unit and confirm their self-worth. Family time could take the form of a family chill-out night, with all the duvets from the beds brought downstairs, an indoor picnic with the child's favourite food and a DVD of their choice, or it could be a weekly visit to the cinema or bowling alley – something that involves all of the family and reassures the child that they have support and love.

Increase affection

More kisses, cuddles and reassurances that you love them are very important in confirming to your child that they are deserving of love. Give them all the high-vibrational energy you can. This will impart a feeling of security and improve their emotional stability. Try to make affection a part of normal life: a hug when they get out of the bath, a cuddle up with a story book before they go to bed. This will help to raise their frequency before they settle for the night and keep away negative thoughts about bullying, which could cause restless nights and tiredness the next day. You can't tell your child often enough that you love them. This is the best way to teach them that they are deserving of love.

Praise and appreciation

It is very important to recognise your child's achievements and to let them know how proud they have made you. When they bring home their school report, always pick out the good things that they have done and tell them how proud you are; focus on what they have achieved. If there are negatives that need to be pointed out, this should be done in a light manner at the end and not made a priority.

Praise your child for everything they do that is positive – tidying their room, clearing the table, washing up, cleaning the car, doing their homework on time – as this confirms to them that you care about them. Giving them praise is in effect giving them high-vibrational energy, which helps to programme their subconscious mind to believe that they deserve it. The more love they believe they deserve, the higher their average vibrational frequency will be. The more you do, especially when they are young, to show that they deserve love in their life, the better emotionally equipped they will be to handle the attention of a bully.

Compliment them
Letting your child know that you are thinking of them is very important, and paying them compliments is an excellent way of doing this. Make a point of mentioning when you feel they look nice: it could be their clothes, their hair, the colours they are wearing or even their image. This will all help to lift their frequency and make them feel better about themselves.

Communicate with them
Be interested in your child's life: ask about their day, engage them in conversation and set aside a time each day when you talk. If they seem reluctant to talk about certain areas of their life, then allow them their space; they will open up to you when they are ready. The very fact that you are interested in their life will show them that you care, which, again, will help to raise their energy frequency.

Involve them in family decisions
Where possible, let your child have input when it comes to family decisions, such as where to go on holiday, what colour to paint the living room or what type of television set to buy. The act of involving them makes them feel

appreciated and important, confirming to them yet again that they deserve love.

Give them responsibility
Look at the workings of your household and try to give some of the responsibilities to your child. Perhaps they can look after the hamster, or feed the rabbit, or be in charge of the rota for using the internet. Giving them responsibilities will show them that you trust them and believe in them, which in turn will give them more confidence in themselves and ultimately help raise their energy frequency.

If You Are the Bully ...

We have already established that, living in a world of energy as we do, anything that generates low-vibrational energy is harmful to us all.

We have focused on how you can stop a bully hurting you or your child, but the bully also needs help in order to break the cycle. Perhaps you are yourself a bully and now want to do something about it. Or perhaps you are in a position to help someone else improve their vibrational energy and stop using bullying tactics.

Understanding the background

If you are behaving in a bullying manner, it is more than likely that you have been bullied yourself at some time, so you too are a victim and need help to understand what is happening to you. Perhaps up until now you have been unaware of what you are doing and the negative impact you are having on others, as well as on yourself.

Since the programming probably goes back to your early childhood, it may not be possible for you to identify immediately where your low-vibrational energies originate from, but thinking or talking about your childhood may offer a clue. Perhaps you had an overbearing father, or something happened to make you feel inferior to everybody else. A parent may have left the family home; your parents may not have shown you much affection; you may even have been abused. Once you can understand the cause of your current behaviour, you can take steps to rectify it.

Helping yourself

If you have recognised yourself as a bully, you will probably already be able to see ways of helping yourself to stop behaving in this destructive way. The key is to start with small actions. Each step you take will encourage higher-vibrational energies and discourage lower ones, slowly enabling you to build your self-esteem. Try the following ideas:

▸ If you find yourself criticising someone, stop. Say nothing, or say something nice instead.
▸ If you feel over-protective towards someone and don't want them to talk to anyone else, organise a three-way conversation.
▸ Try asking someone else to make the decision about what you do or which film you go to see.
▸ If someone disagrees with your point of view, try putting yourself in their shoes and seeing things from another perspective. You may not always be right.
▸ Practise saying 'Yes, okay' in front of the mirror.

Consider your comfort zone too. Think about where you feel comfortable in your life and make a list of your own expectations. Now add to the top of your list:

▸ I expect to feel good about myself and be thoughtful towards the people around me.

The reason for your bullying behaviour may be the effect of other people's behaviour on you long ago, but it's down to you – and only you – to change it. Just because you have been a bully in the past, it doesn't mean you have to go on being a bully in the present. You *can* change your behaviour.

Three Steps to a Bully-free Life

The final sections of the book focus on the fundamental issue of raising your average vibrational energy level. It is your action plan for changing your life.

To prevent bullying from remaining in your life, you have to look at your thinking processes and make the necessary changes. This means re-programming your subconscious mind to believe that you do not attract bullies into your life. In HVT terms, that entails raising your average energy frequency level in a permanent way, and changing your comfort zone in the process.

The aim of the exercises in the remainder of the book is to help you to become more high-frequency in your general thinking and eliminate any low-frequency thought patterns that you may have been carrying. This will have the effect of increasing your personal energy frequency, which in turn will push the barriers of your comfort zone. There are three steps in this process:

- ▶ Step 1: accept responsibility for your life.
- ▶ Step 2: make the commitment to eradicate bullies from your life.
- ▶ Step 3: undertake a six-week programme of practical exercises to re-programme your subconscious mind.

Step 1: Accepting responsibility

If a bully is active in your life, this is only happening because at some level of your subconscious mind you believe it can. In my view, probably about 99 per cent of us believe that we can be bullied, as in one way or another bullying touches nearly every one of us.

The act of accepting responsibility for what happens in our lives empowers. It gives us the control that we need to be able to do something about our situation. If we don't accept responsibility, we are in effect giving our power away and blaming outside factors for what happens in our life. It is vital to accept the fact that you are in control and can do something to enable you to move forward in a positive and constructive way.

Step 2: Making the commitment

You must be totally committed to changing your life for the better if you really want to move forward and eradicate bullies from your life once and for all. A very strange thing happens when you truly commit to something – you tap into an extraordinary force that raises your levels of power and control beyond what you would normally expect.

Step 3: Undertaking the programme

Nothing is achieved without work, but it is not difficult to work through the simple exercises I provide in the following pages. If you repeat them regularly, they will make a huge difference to your life. In addition to the small steps you have been taking so far, I will take you through some proven and powerful affirmation and visualisation exercises designed to raise the frequency of your personal energy field on a permanent basis.

Your self-improvement programme

The programme for self-improvement I am setting you is to be followed over a six-week period, which in my experience is the optimum period to initiate change. However, I strongly recommend that you repeat this six-week module four times, with a one-week rest period in between each of the six-week modules. This will take you a total of 27 weeks, which is the six months that I personally found cemented permanent change.

This is what you will have to do:

▸ Make a statement of your acceptance of responsibility and repeat it as often as you like.
▸ Make a commitment to stopping bullying in your life and repeat it as often as you like.
▸ Dedicate your commitment to someone special to you.
▸ Read the high-vibrational affirmation you have been given for the first week and then write five more of your own.
▸ Repeat the week's affirmations ten times in the morning and ten times in the evening every day.
▸ Use a visualisation exercise every day. I have provided the first two; you need to develop four more of your own.

All this should take you ten or fifteen minutes a day – not much when the results will change your life!

Use the timetable on pages 119–25 to monitor your progress, ticking off the exercises as you do them. This will help you to stay focused and bring an element of discipline to your programme.

Accepting Responsibility

If you don't admit that there are issues you want to change, you will never succeed in changing them. Once you have accepted responsibility for what is happening in your life, you will have the control to do something about it.

The act of acceptance will also make you aware of a whole host of low-vibrational thought patterns. These flourish in a mind that gives its power away. 'Poor me', 'Why am I so unlucky?', 'Everybody is against me', 'It's not my fault' – we are all guilty of these kinds of thoughts, but it is essential to try to avoid them. They are low-vibrational and serve only one purpose: that is, to drag down your energy frequency, making life much harder for you. You are much more likely to attract the attention of a bully in this vulnerable state of mind. So, as you can see, step one is vitally important. You cannot move forward until you have acknowledged that you are responsible for your life.

Your acceptance statement
Think carefully about your decision to accept that you are responsible for your life and put it in writing. This will strengthen your belief. You can either copy the following acceptance statement, filling in the date and your name, or write your own.

*From today, the .... of .... 20...,
I, ..., accept full responsibility for my
life. I realise that there is no point in holding on to any low-
vibrational feelings and emotions from the past. I release any
negative energy that I am holding on to. From this moment I
accept total responsibility.*

Strengthen yourself every day

Repeat your acceptance statement out loud to yourself
several times. As you do so, see yourself letting go of all
your low-vibrational energy and allowing your energy
frequency to rise as you move your life forward into a new
and exciting future.

Read through your acceptance statement every
morning, as many times as you like, and any time you feel
your old low-vibrational feelings creeping back.

Making the Commitment

Being totally committed to raising your energy profile will give you extraordinary power. The dramatist Goethe wrote:

> *The moment one commits oneself, then providence moves too. All sorts of things occur to help one that would never have otherwise occurred. A whole new stream of events, all manner of unforeseen incidents and chance meetings, and material assistance come forth which no one could have dreamt would appear.*

Something quite magical occurs when we make a committed decision. When our intention is totally focused, we tap into the incredible power of the subconscious mind and enlist its full support in our chosen endeavour. Normally, the subconscious mind sticks to its comfort zone, placing restrictions on our intentions and achievements. However, when our commitment is total, we seem to be able to override subconscious programming and access its incredible potential. If you commit completely, then the possibility of failure is not even a consideration.

What real commitment can achieve

I remember a story a policeman told me about a car accident he attended one night. A young child was trapped under one of the cars and four burly policemen were attempting to lift the car off the child. They struggled without success; the car was just too heavy to move. Then the mother of the child took hold of the car and lifted it off the child by herself. The policemen looked on in amazement at what seemed impossible. What had happened was that the woman had totally committed herself to lifting the car, and her focused commitment had overridden her programming about what was and wasn't possible.

The act of commitment overrides limitations created by our belief system, by society and by our upbringing and enables us to reach our true potential. Once Roger Bannister had broken the four-minute mile and proved that what had been seen as impossible was, in fact, possible, four or five other athletes broke his record within weeks.

The deeper your commitment, the fewer problems your subconscious programming will cause you. You must leave no exit strategies, allow no 'maybes' or attitudes of 'we will

You must be totally committed to eradicating bullies from your life once and for all.

103

see how it goes'. This is a sure-fire way of guaranteeing failure. You must focus on success – nothing else will do.

Your commitment

You will find that six weeks is a comfortable time period in which to stay focused on your goal, determined and in control without too much interference from your subconscious mind.

Think carefully about your commitment to what you want to achieve. Then either copy the following commitment statement, filling in the date and your name, or write your own.

From today, the .... of .... 20...,
I, ..., commit to focus on my goal with all my strength for the next six weeks. I will succeed in my desire to carry out the exercises and disciplines required, and I will not fail.

Now read your commitment statement out loud as many times as you like. Any time you feel your willpower beginning to weaken, refer back to your dedication to reinforce your commitment.

Dedicate your commitment

A good way to reinforce your commitment is to dedicate your goal to somebody special to you, perhaps your son or daughter, your mother or father, or your partner. It also helps if you can put the dedication in writing, so that you can refer back to it in moments of weakness. Write down the name of the person and why you are choosing them for your dedication. This may simply be because you love them, or it may be because you want to be able to be more supportive towards them or because you respect them and want to be more like them.

I, ..., dedicate the following six weeks to
.... because ....
...
I will make you very proud of me.

This act of dedication will help to sustain you when your subconscious starts complaining and your determination and willpower weaken.

Making progress

It took me personally six months to make real permanent changes within my life, although this may not necessarily be the case for you. However, it will take some time, and that means plenty of opportunities for your subconscious mind to find ways to sabotage your efforts. Watch out for thoughts that are counter-productive to your goal. I found that my subconscious went very quiet for a couple of weeks when faced with failure; then, when I had become complacent in my focus, it suddenly reappeared and was back to its old tricks!

You will know you are really beginning to succeed when quite suddenly you find that the effort you have had to summon up on a daily basis to push towards your desired goal lessens and perhaps even disappears.

Think what it's like when you first join a gym. Your initial enthusiasm propels you through the first few visits. Then your subconscious starts to get bored and begins to find reasons for you to stay at home. If you persist and become healthier, it no longer recognises the new you as fitting in its comfort zone and tries to keep you at the lower frequency level where it feels you belong. But if you keep going nevertheless, one day you will suddenly realise that you can't face life without going to the gym. In fact, if you don't go, you will probably feel down and lethargic. This is your new comfort zone – and this one is good for you!

This process is one that we go through whenever we wish to make positive changes in our life. The trick is to understand what is going on in your own mind. This will enable you to stay committed to your goal and in control of your subconscious mind. You must show it who is boss.

Your Affirmations

I recommend two main methods for helping you raise your energy profile: affirmation and visualisation. Both are really simple and so are easy to put into practice. They rely for their power on repetition, and – believe me – they are a powerful way to change your life.

A high-vibrational energy field vibrates faster and expands out much further than a low-vibrational energy field.

The advantage of these techniques is that they can be used in small corners of your day and so don't need to impact detrimentally on your routine. If you want to, you can do them quietly on your own and no-one else need be involved. This can be a real help in building up your personal strength and raising your vibrational energy levels in order to help you take action to stop that bully.

Positive affirmations

Affirmations are powerful statements that you repeat to yourself so often that you persuade your subconscious mind to accept them as being true. If you continually bombard yourself with these statements, you will reprogramme your subconscious mind, thus redefining the boundaries of your comfort zone. Obviously, you need to use powerful high-vibrational statements, which you can tailor to your own particular needs. This will have the effect of replacing low-vibrational thought patterns with high-vibrational thought patterns and raising the frequency of your personal energy field. The longer you keep this up, the more permanent the rise in frequency will be.

As we have already seen, your life will run a lot more smoothly at the higher frequency levels, so it makes sense to pursue with vigour any methods you have at your disposal to achieve a higher vibrational level.

Writing your affirmations

Here are some examples of affirmations you might use. You can choose anything that strengthens your purpose and brings positive energy into your life.

- ▸ I love and approve of myself.
- ▸ I repel bullies from my life.
- ▸ I am confident and strong.
- ▸ I radiate powerful positive energy.

▸ I have a powerful presence.
▸ I am in control of my life.
▸ Bullies do not intimidate me.
▸ I am free from bullying.
▸ I will not be bullied today.
▸ I am a wonderful person.

Affirmations should be written in the present tense, as if you have already attained them. Don't admit of any doubts.

You could write your affirmations on flash cards and keep them in your purse or wallet. Or stick them somewhere where you will see them as you go about your day, for example on the fridge.

Using your affirmations
Each week you will read, preferably out loud, six high-vibrational affirmations. Read them ten times every morning and ten times every night, just before you go to sleep. Use the same affirmations for the course of a week, then move on to the next set of six. Keep repeating your favourite affirmations to yourself all day long whenever you can find the time. After a couple of weeks you will be amazed at how different you feel.

Sometimes, after three to four weeks, you may feel that the affirmations are not really working any more. Don't let this deter you. This is a crucial point, at which you must keep up the bombardment of high-vibrational energy. Your subconscious mind can be very clever and will use all of its persuasive powers to convince you to desist. Do not give in. Keep going. The boundaries of your comfort zone are changing without you realising it. After six weeks you will have made noticeable progress.

At the end of the first six-week period, you may want to change some of your statements before you begin your next six-week course of affirmations.

If you really believe in something, you'll be on the way to achieving it.

Believe me, you can't bombard your subconscious mind enough! You should live and breathe high-vibrational thoughts. They will push up the frequency of your personal energy field, changing your life for the better in the process. The more high-vibrational thoughts you think, the more used to them your mind will become. You are drowning out the low-vibrational thoughts, not allowing them to take hold and drag down your personal energy frequency. If you do this enough, your subconscious mind will accept that this higher frequency state is the norm for you, and then this will become your natural state of being.

Your Visualisations

Walt Disney said, 'If you can dream it, you can do it.' That's what visualisation is all about.

Visualisation is a powerful tool, which you can use to help reprogramme your subconscious mind. What you are doing is convincing your subconscious mind that you are capable of achieving the subject of your visualisation. The secret to success in any area of life is to believe that you can do it, or – to be more precise – to make your subconscious mind believe that you can do it. As the real source of your unlimited potential lies within your subconscious mind, this is where your true capabilities lie.

Visualisation can help you to mould your expectations to your advantage.

Belief is the key to success, as to truly believe eliminates any doubts from your mind and moves you into a frequency zone where anything is possible. This is the zone where you are calm, happy, and detached from the outcome of your objective (becoming over-involved could open the door to doubt and pull your frequency level down into a less productive zone). The secret is to relax, know that you will succeed, and trust in your ability; just enjoy the moment and bask in the high vibrations. Then, almost without thinking about your objective, allow everything to flow naturally. Success will be almost guaranteed.

How to visualise

A visualisation is simply a high-powered daydream! You just need get comfortable, relax and launch your imagination. Learn to see yourself in positive situations in which bullies avoid you. They don't want to confront you, because they realise that you are strong and focused. If you see yourself as a person whom bullies won't go near, this will become your comfort zone. Remember, you have only to believe in something to make it a reality.

The key to successful visualisation is your imagination: learn to use it to your advantage. See yourself in successful situations, whether they relate to work, relationships or leisure. The more you use visualisation, the better you will become at it and the easier it will be for your subconscious to accept the visualisation as real. Truly believing something will make it happen.

Your visualisation programme

For this programme, you should do a visualisation exercise every day for the six-week period. The best time is when you wake up in the morning, as this will set your energy levels on high vibration for the remainder of the day. Each visualisation takes about five minutes.

I have provided two visualisations. Use these for the first two weeks and then create a new one yourself for each following week. Visualisation is much more effective if you incorporate things that are personal to you. Include anything that makes you feel good about yourself. Make space in your timetable to plan and write your visualisation exercises.

Comfort your inner child visualisation

Your life is merely a reflection of what your subconscious mind believes you desire. As we have already noted, our subconscious mind is also known as our inner child, because it has all the attributes and characteristics of a small child. As you know, it has an established comfort zone, which is the way it is programmed to think life should be for you and where it wants you to remain. Whether this is good or bad for you is irrelevant, as your inner child cannot differentiate between the two.

Comforting your inner child is beneficial to many areas of your life. It allows you to acknowledge the importance of your subconscious while at the same time letting go of any low-vibrational thought patterns that may have taken root there, perhaps some time ago. When looking to move your life forward, it is important to clear out these low-frequency feelings and emotions, otherwise they will hold you back and hamper your progress as if you were carrying a dead weight.

This exercise can sometimes unearth deep emotional issues from the past. Of course, that is what we are trying to achieve, but if you feel in any way apprehensive about this, it may be helpful to have somebody sit with you the first few times you do this visualisation. Then they can offer support and reassurance if necessary. You might like to have them read through the visualisation first to help you work through it.

*Comforting your inner child shows them that you love them;
when your inner child feels loved, they will be much more
helpful to you as you negotiate life's hurdles.*

The point of this exercise is to see your inner child
happy and having fun, and most of all to reassure them
that you love them. Loving your inner child will help you
to release any deep-seated low-vibrational thought patterns
that may be embedded in your mind.
You can adapt the visualisation in any way you like to
make it more personal to you.

The stages of the visualisation are as follows:

▸ Read through the visualisation first so you understand
  what it is trying to achieve and what you need to do.
▸ Get yourself comfortable in a warm room, in a
  comfortable chair or on your bed.
▸ Close your eyes and relax.
▸ Slowly run through the visualisation in your mind.
▸ Once you have completed the visualisation, lie and relax
  until you are ready to return to the real world again.

The visualisation

Imagine that you are making contact with your inner child for the first time.

Picture a situation in which somebody is bullying you. See this person being aggressive to you, feel the emotions present. You feel fear. You hear the intensity in their voice and you feel uncertain as to how to react. Now turn round and look behind you. Standing there is your inner child – that's you at five years old – hiding behind you. Look at your inner child and see the look of fear on their face.

Take a deep breath, bend down and pick up the child. Hold them close to you and comfort them. See how the child feels reassured and calms down, and the fear seems to lift.

Now turn to face the bully. The determination is written all over your face. You have had enough. This is not going to happen to you again. The bully looks at you and you see the look of fear on their face. They know you are focused and determined. They appear nervous and edgy. You look them directly in the eye and say to them, 'That's enough. You will never speak to me like that again and you will never upset this lovely child again. Now get out of my life and do not return.'

Watch as the bully drops his shoulders and, head down, walks away, not daring to turn around. Keep watching as he disappears into the distance. Know deep in your heart that he will never return.

Now hold your inner child and give them a big hug. See the smile appear on their face and pull them close to you, giving them a gentle kiss on the cheek. Say to your inner child, 'I am sorry that I allowed that to happen to us, but I promise you that from this day on it will never happen again. I will always be here to look after you, and I love you very much.' See the look of joy spread across your inner child's face as you cuddle and kiss them again; feel the love between you both and enjoy the beautiful feelings evoked. Put your inner child down on the grass and hold their hand as you both run off across

*the field, laughing. Feel a powerful bond of love growing
between you. You are both so happy.*

Enjoying your inner child visualisation

This is the second visualisation exercise. It is, again,
intended to help you get in touch with your inner child.
Remember, you can adapt it however you like to suit you.
The aim is to get in touch with your subconscious and feel
good about yourself. Don't forget to spend a few minutes
relaxing and coming slowly back to the real world after
you have finished your visualisation.

The visualisation

*It's a beautiful sunny day. You are gazing out of the bedroom
window across green fields. In one of the fields you can see
horses running playfully, enjoying the warm sunshine. The
horses display such vitality as they run that it fills you with
joy just watching them.*

*You decide to go out for a walk and set off down the stairs
to the back door. As you reach the bottom of the stairs, you see
a small child sitting on the floor playing with some toys. It is
you at five years old: your inner child. 'Come on, let's go for a
walk,' you say. Your inner child smiles from ear to ear as they
jump up and take hold of your hand.*

*When you walk outside, the warmth of the sun hits you
and you feel happy and alive. Your inner child runs off
giggling, overcome with joy. You chase after them, and they try
to run away from you, laughing and screaming. You sweep
them up into your arms, giving them a big hug and kiss on the
cheek. 'I love you,' you say, as you hold them close, feeling the
warmth of the love between you.*

*The birdsong seems louder than ever today. The horses see
you near the fence and come trotting over. 'Watch me feed the
horses,' you say to your inner child, pulling up a handful of
grass. As the horses gently munch on the grass, your inner*

child looks on in amazement. 'Stroke the horse,' you say, gently taking your inner child's hand and rubbing it on the horse's head. You are both so happy together. You explain to your inner child that you love them very much and you will always be there to love and take care of them.

You tell your inner child that you are going to do a six-week programme that will make life much better for you both. It will help you get a better job and have a happier life. Explain that this also means you will be able to buy a new wide-screen television and go on more holidays. See your inner child happy at your announcement and excited about the future. Set off back to the house, both you and the child very happy and content with life.

Visualisation in daily life

Now that you have made contact with your inner child, you may find it beneficial to keep up the relationship. Visualisation is a wonderful way of doing this. You can use it whenever you have a few spare moments in your day. You can also use visualisation in other areas of your life. For example, you may want to use it to help with your job. Set aside five minutes each day to visualise how you want your work day to go; put negative thoughts out of your mind and imagine the best scenario. You may want to use visualisation to improve your relationships. Use your imagination to play out any scene that you feel will help. See yourself and your partner in happy, loving situations. Remember, you just have to truly believe it and this is what you will get.

Practice is the key here. The more often you visualise, the more readily your subconscious mind will accept your visualisations. This will enable you to run through any bullying visualisations that you feel may be appropriate whenever you need them, as practice will have honed your skills, making your subconscious mind open to your suggestions. Visualisation puts you in the driving seat, enabling you to control your subconscious mind rather than it controlling you.

As you use HVT in your life, you will become increasingly aware of the constant tussle taking place between your conscious and your subconscious mind. When you notice this taking place, it may help to spend a little time explaining to your subconscious mind what it is that you are trying to achieve. Make your inner child part of your life and remember your life will be a lot easier if you can enlist their support in your endeavours. Explain to them the benefits to both of you of what you are doing. Don't forget that they are a child and make it attractive to them. For example, if you are a student taking exams and feeling unsure of your capabilities, ask your inner child to help you. Explain that if you pass your exams, you will be able to get a better, higher-paid job, which means more treats, such as a trip to the zoo or a new computer game. Remember, you are trying to motivate a five-year-old child, so think in terms of what they would like.

Learning to communicate with your inner child is important if you are really to move forward and fully realise your amazing potential. After all, it is the thought patterns that are programmed into the mind of your inner child that dominate your life. In order to make changes in this area it is vital first of all to open the channels of communication.

My Progress to a Bully-free Life

Use these pages to write your own affirmations, make notes on your personal visualisations and tick off when you have completed your tasks. It will help to keep you on track, give you focus and purpose, and also reassure you that things are improving all the time.

My acceptance statement

. . . .
. . . .
. . . .
. . . .

My commitment statement

. . . .
. . . .
. . . .
. . . .

My dedication

. . . .
. . . .
. . . .
. . . .

Week 1
My affirmations

▸ I love and approve of myself.

▸ . . . .

▸ . . . .

▸ . . . .

▸ . . . .

▸ . . . .

My visualisation

▸ Comfort your inner child visualisation (see pages 115–6).

My checklist

Day	Morning affirmations	Visualisation	Evening affirmations
Monday			
Tuesday			
Wednesday			
Thursday			
Friday			
Saturday			
Sunday			

Week 2
My affirmations

▶ I repel bullies from my life.

▶ . . . .

▶ . . . .

▶ . . . .

▶ . . . .

▶ . . . .

My visualisation

▶ Enjoying your inner child visualisation (see pages 116–7).

My checklist

Day	Morning affirmations	Visualisation	Evening affirmations
Monday			
Tuesday			
Wednesday			
Thursday			
Friday			
Saturday			
Sunday			

Week 3
My affirmations

▸ I am confident and strong.

▸ ....

▸ ....

▸ ....

▸ ....

▸ ....

My visualisation

▸ ....

My checklist

Day	Morning affirmations	Visualisation	Evening affirmations
Monday			
Tuesday			
Wednesday			
Thursday			
Friday			
Saturday			
Sunday			

Week 4
My affirmations

▸ I radiate powerful positive energy.

▸ . . . .

▸ . . . .

▸ . . . .

▸ . . . .

▸ . . . .

My visualisation

▸ . . . .

My checklist

Day	Morning affirmations	Visualisation	Evening affirmations
Monday			
Tuesday			
Wednesday			
Thursday			
Friday			
Saturday			
Sunday			

Week 5
My affirmations

▸ I have a powerful presence.

▸ . . . .

▸ . . . .

▸ . . . .

▸ . . . .

▸ . . . .

My visualisation

▸ . . . .

My checklist

Day	*Morning affirmations*	*Visualisation*	*Evening affirmations*
Monday			
Tuesday			
Wednesday			
Thursday			
Friday			
Saturday			
Sunday			

Week 6
My affirmations

▶ I am in control of my life.

▶ ....

▶ ....

▶ ....

▶ ....

▶ ....

My visualisation

▶ ....

My checklist

Day	Morning affirmations	Visualisation	Evening affirmations
Monday			
Tuesday			
Wednesday			
Thursday			
Friday			
Saturday			
Sunday			

Index

abusive relationships 87
acceptance of responsibility 98
awareness of low-vibrational
   thought patterns 100
   statement 100–1, 119
   strengthen yourself every day 101
   see also affirmations,
      visualisation techniques
affection for child, increasing 92
affirmations
   first, to change your life 79, 83
   making personal 88–9, 90
   positive 108–10
   raising energy profile 107
   using your 109–110
   writing down 108–9
appreciation for child 92–3
arrogance 25
atoms 8–9

Bannister, Roger (athlete) 103
bills
   how to stop worrying about 54–5
blame, avoiding 26
boasting 60
breaking cycle of bullying 79–85
   first affirmation to change your
      life 79–80
   it's not your problem 81
   let comments pass you by 82
   return to sender 82–3
   spot the bully and avoid
      them 80–1
   stand tall and smarten up 84
   stand up for yourself 83–4
   turn the conversation on its
      head 84–5
bullies

comfort zone of 96
helping yourself 96–7
how friends can be 69–71
subconscious and attracting
   attention of 87–8
understanding the
   background 95–6
vibrational level of 58–9, 74, 81
who are they? 67, 69–74
bully-free life, three steps to 97–9
   step 1: accepting responsibility 98
   step 2: making commitment 98,
      119
   step 3: undertaking the
      programme 98
bullying
   boasting and 60
   breaking cycle 79–85
   damage caused to environment 64
   definition of 5–6, 68
   effect on bullied 5–6, 68
   effect on bully 6, 58
   prevalence of 5
   start of 61–2
   as vicious circle 62–3
   at work 71–2
   why do they pick on me? 65–6
   your reaction to 68
bullying at school
   effect on victims 73–4, 75,
   talking to teachers 77
   talking to your child 77, 78
   types of 73
   what parents should look for 76–7

change
   6-week optimum period to
      initiate 99, 109

comfort zone
of bullies 96
definition 22
and dieting 28–9, 51–2
effect of positive affirmations 108
HVT as way of reprogramming your 51–3, 86–90
and keeping fit 30–1
and life of crime 27–8
power of subconscious 87
re-evaluate yourself 90
and similar backgrounds 31–6
subconscious mind preference 20, 22–25
take it a step at a time 89
you are worth it! 88–9
commitment
dedication of 104–5
how subconscious may sabotage 105–6
importance of 98, 102–4
statement of 104, 119
communicating with child 93
complimenting child 93
concentrating on moment 55–6
conscious mind 18, subconscious mind ('inner child')
conversation, changing the 84–5

dieting 28
drug addiction 17

emotional energy
differing frequencies of high and low 10, 13–15
see also emotional frequency, personal energy
emotional frequency
avoid blaming others 26
comfort zone 22–4
conscious mind and 18
daily fluctuation 39–48
effect of subconscious mind 23–5, 27–36
formative years 20–2
how it is established 18–26
location 39
not better but different 25
other people's effect on 37–8
subconscious mind and 18–20
energy
people as part of exchange of 9–10
world as an ocean of 8–9
see also emotional energy, high-vibrational energy, low-vibrational energy
envy 25

family decision-making 93–4
family time 92
fear 13–14, 15
friends who are bullies 70–1

happiness 14–15
high vibrational thinking (HVT)
automatic benefits of 10–12, 21
changing your life 10, 50–1, 53–4, 109–10
coping with negative energy 49
definition 9–10
effects on home and work 12, 35–6
focus on the present moment 54–5
life runs more smoothly 11, 21, 108
one step at a time 55
simplicity of 12
to increase personal energy 17
to reprogramme subconscious 51–3
taking control using 50–1

love 13–14, 20–1, 50, 63, 92
low-vibrational energy
bullying and 74
definition of 54
recognise and reject 54–5
thought patterns 100

mirror visualisation technique 82–3
misbehaviour, bullying related 73–4, 75
molecules 9

parents' help for their child *see* raising child's energy level
personal energy field
daily fluctuations 39–48
effect of emotion on 14–15
focus on present moment, 55–7

how we try to increase vibration of 15–17
stand tall and smarten up 84
take one step at a time 57
see also emotional frequency, high-vibrational energy
picking on people 70
positive feelings 15
praise and appreciation for child 92–3
present moment, focus on 55–7

radio waves 14
raising child's energy level
communicating with them 93
family home-life 91
giving them responsibility 94
increasing affection 92
increasing family time 92
involvement in family decisions 93–4
paying compliments 93
praise and appreciation 92–3
responsibility given to child 94
return negativity to sender 82–3

school
bullying at 72–4
see also bullying
self-criticism 25
self-importance 25
self-improvement programme
6-week period to initiate change 99
checklist to help follow 120–5
time needed 99
timetable 99, 120–5
see also affirmations, commitment, visualisation techniques
stand tall and smarten up 84
stand up for yourself 83–4
subconscious mind ('inner child')
as 5-year-old child 18–20, 31
attracting attention of bullies 86–8
comforting inner child visualisation 113–16
enjoying inner child visualisation 116–17
enlisting help of your 118

HVT to reprogramme comfort zone 51–3, 111–12
personal affirmations 88–9
power of subconscious 87–8, 105–6
re-evaluate yourself 90
sabotaging effects of 24–5, 105–6, 109
self-confirming beliefs of 21
taking it a step at a time 89
see also comfort zone

techniques to break bullying cycle
first affirmation to change life 79–80
it's not your problem 81
let comments pass you by 82
return to sender 82–3
spot and avoid bully 80–1
stand tall and smarten up 84
stand up for yourself 83–4
turn conversation on its head 84–5
see also raising child's energy level
Tesla, Dr Nikola (scientist) 8
turn conversation on its head 84–5

visualisation techniques
6-week programme 112–13
belief as key to success 112
comfort your inner child 113–16
enjoy your inner child 116–17
enlisting your inner child's support 118
how to visualise 112
in daily life 117–18
keep practising 117–18
mirror 82–3
raising your energy level 89
reprogramming subconscious mind 111
specific activities 89

work
boss who is a bully 72
bullying at 71–2